Children's Minds

Margaret Donaldson was educated at the MacLaren High School, Callander, Perthshire, and at the University of Edinburgh, where she has continued as a teacher since ceasing to be a student and where she is now a Reader in Psychology. In spite of her attachment to Edinburgh, however, she has made frequent visits elsewhere. She spent a term in Piaget's research institute in Geneva and a year in the United States as the holder of a John Hay Whitney Fellowship. She has returned to the States to lecture on a number of subsequent occasions; and during several summers she worked there with Bruner on curriculum development projects. She is the author of *A Study of Children's Thinking* and of numerous journal articles.

Children's Minds

Margaret Donaldson

FONTANA/CROOM HELM

© 1978 Margaret Donaldson
Croom Helm Ltd, 2-10 St John's Road, London SW11

British Library Cataloguing in Publication Data

Donaldson, Margaret
   Children's minds.
   1. Child psychology 2. Learning, Psychology of
   I. Title
   155.4'13   LB1139.L/

   ISBN 0-85664-759-4

Printed in Great Britain by
Biddles Ltd, Guildford, Surrey

Contents

Contents

Dedicated to the memory of
James McGarrigle

Preface

In the course of this book I argue that the evidence now compels us to reject certain features of Jean Piaget's theory of intellectual development. It may seem odd, then, if my first acknowledgement of indebtedness is to a man whose work I criticize. Yet the indebtedness is there and the acknowledgement is certainly due. Many years ago he was kind enough to welcome me to the Institut des Sciences de l'Education in Geneva; and much of my subsequent research was stimulated by the excitement of that first visit. If I must now reject some of his teaching, no lessening of respect for the man or for his vast contribution to knowledge is implied. No theory in science is final; and no one is more fully aware of this than Piaget himself. I should add further that, while the early chapters of the book propose certain re-interpretations, much that is said later is, I believe, in no way incompatible with Piaget's views and has certainly been influenced by them in positive ways.

During the last ten or twelve years, I have had the good fortune to work in Edinburgh with a number of extremely able colleagues and graduate students. In the mid-1960s I began a study of pre-school children in collaboration with Roger Wales, George Balfour, Robin Campbell, John Taylor and Brian Young; and Eve Curme also worked with us for a while before she married Herbert Clark and went to America, to our considerable loss. Later, as members of the original group left, others came: Robert Grieve, Barbara Wallington, Peter Lloyd, Michael Garman, Patrick Griffiths, Lesley Hall,

9

Martin Hughes, James McGarrigle and Alison Macrae. I have made extensive use of research by members of this group in developing the arguments of the book, and I gained much from the exchange of ideas with all of them over the years. I also remember with gratitude the visitors from other parts of the world who joined us for longer or shorter periods of time and greatly enriched us by their company.

It is never possible to acknowledge – or even be conscious of – all the influences on one's thinking. But there is one influence which must, I think, be evident: that of Jerome Bruner, with his deep concern about the links between psychology and education and his rare capacity for translating concern into effective action. I was privileged to work in Cambridge, Massachusetts, as a member of various groups of people whom he brought together in the attempt to understand better how children learn and how they may be helped to learn. This book owes much to that experience.

It would be a serious omission if, returning now in thought to Edinburgh, I were to fail to speak of the children in our departmental research nursery and of the staff – Muriel Slade and Noveen Strachan – who run it so competently; or of Janet Panther, our secretary, on whose efficiency and cheerfulness we continually – and with complete safety – rely.

Several people – Robin Campbell, Martin Hughes, Alison Macrae, Jess Reid and my husband, Stephen Salter – have read the manuscript of this book in its earlier stages. I am grateful to all of them for the care they have taken in doing so, for their thoughtful comments and for many helpful discussions.

Finally I want to thank the Social Science Research Council for the Personal Research Grant which allowed me to spend a year thinking and writing in peace.

Note: While the word 'child' does not convey any information as to sex, there is no similarly neutral personal pronoun in English. I have followed here, though not without some heart-searching, the tradition of using the masculine form 'he' when a neutral sense is intended. It is particularly desirable when one is speaking of education not to suggest that boys are somehow more important. The arguments in this book apply equally to boys and to girls.

Prologue

The scene is a small open courtyard, within a school building. There are paving stones, warm in the sunshine, and tubs bright with flowers. On top of a low wall a child is lying, propped up on her elbows, looking at a book with intense concentration. Near her another child is carefully watering the flowers, while a third is sitting with his back against the wall and a notebook on his knees. He appears to be drawing or writing something. Like the first child, he is lost in his task.

All around the courtyard, inside the building, there are pleasant carpeted areas where many children are busily occupied in a variety of ways, while teachers wander among them, talking to them, smiling at them, encouraging their efforts.

As I watched this scene on a morning in May 1977, it occurred to me that a visitor to the school who knew nothing about our society might have been inclined to think he had found Utopia, especially if he had been told that the children he was watching came from families living in a somewhat underprivileged part of one of our large cities.

Letting my mind play with this thought, I then wondered how it would seem to the visitor if he were to go on to observe the behaviour and conversation of children in certain classes at the other end of our educational system – the older brothers and sisters of these same children perhaps, about to take their leave of school for ever and heartily thankful to have done with it. And I imagined him reading our newspapers and listening to our television programmes with their recurring cries of educational woe: falling standards, illiterate and innumerate adolescents pouring forth from the schools in their thousands, not fitted to earn a living in the kind of world they must enter, discontented, disillusioned, defeated before they have begun.

The visitor would certainly soon have abandoned the notion that he had found Utopia. But he would also surely have been very perplexed to understand what goes wrong.

1. The School Experience

Where attainable knowledge could have changed
the issue, ignorance has the guilt of vice.
(A. N. Whitehead.)

And nature has no use for the plea that one 'did not
know'. Not knowing acts like guilt. (C. G. Jung.)

When we make laws which compel our children to go to
school we assume collectively an awesome responsibility. For
a period of some ten years, with minor variations from country
to country, the children are conscripts; and their youth does
nothing to alter the seriousness of this fact. Nor is it altered by
the intention, however genuine, that the school experience
should be 'for their good'.

I am not among those who advocate what has come to be
known as 'deschooling society'. I believe that we need schools
– and never more than now. But the justification of a long
enforced period of national service is not something we can
treat lightly. The question that must be asked, and considered
seriously, and reconsidered as knowledge and circumstances
change, is whether the school experience really *is* good for
our children – as good as we could make it. And this, of
course, amounts to the same thing as asking whether it really
is good for the society that will come into being when the
present one is gone.

We are faced now with something of a puzzle. In the first
few years at school all appears to go very well. The children
seem eager, lively, happy. There is commonly an atmosphere
of spontaneity in which they are encouraged to explore and
discover and create. There is much concern, on the part of the
teachers, with high educational ideals. These things tend to be
true even in parts of the community which are far from being
socially privileged in other ways. However, when we consider what has happened by the time the children reach

adolescence, we are forced to recognize that the promise of the early years frequently remains unfulfilled. Large numbers leave school with the bitter taste of defeat in them, not having mastered even moderately well those basic skills which society demands, much less having become people who rejoice in the exercise of creative intelligence.

The problem then is to understand how something that begins so well can often end so badly. And inevitably, faced with this problem, people turn to wondering whether schooling really does begin as well as it seems to do or whether the brightness of the early years carries within itself the shadow of the darkness that is to come.

Thus there is pressure now for change at the lower end of the system. And there is real danger that this pressure might lead to change that would be gravely retrogressive.

In an article in the *Times Educational Supplement* of 24 June 1977, Karl Heinz Gruber urges us not to be so foolish as to throw away what we have gained. He reminds us of these gains by drawing a vivid contrast between our own schools and the elementary schools of continental Europe, which he describes as harsh and rigid places where, from the beginning, children are made anxious – ill, even – by the fear of failure.

We should certainly not go back to that. But having listened to Gruber's warning and alerted ourselves to the risk of loss, we must still ask whether we are doing well enough. For the central problem remains. There is no denying that, in spite of the enlightened concern of our primary schools with happiness, schooling somehow or other turns into a distinctly unhappy experience for many of our children. From it large numbers of them emerge ill-equipped for life in our society and inescapably aware of it. So then either they regard themselves as stupid for failing or else, in an understandable effort to defend against this admission, they regard the activities at which they have failed as stupid. In either event they want no more of these things. How can we justify a long period of national service which ends like that?

For the teachers of unhappy children the school experience is generally unhappy too. For them, however, it is the decision that the pupils are stupid which is the defensive one. They hardly have the option of deciding that the things they teach are stupid, for how then could they justify teaching them? And the only other possibility may seem to be the decision that *they* are the failures.

For society as a whole – or at least that part of society which controls the setting and maintaining of the educational objectives – there are two possible defensive conclusions that may be drawn: either that large numbers of children are indeed irredeemably stupid and must just be written off, or that large numbers of teachers are not doing their jobs properly.

Where does the truth of the matter lie?

The first thing to recognize, in this generally uncomfortable situation, is the extreme difficulty – and in the context of human evolution the extreme novelty – of the educational enterprise which modern Western cultures have taken upon themselves. We need not be too defensive about not yet having managed it well. I shall be arguing later in this book that some of the skills which we value most highly in our educational system are thoroughly alien to the spontaneous modes of functioning of the human mind. And I shall be arguing that the real nature of the problem of developing these skills has not been understood well enough and widely enough.

Defensive postures are usually the enemies of effective action – but so of course is the complacency which can easily replace them if they are abandoned. In the present situation, complacency is disastrous. If we are going to persist in our educational enterprise it is urgent that we learn to do it better. Whatever progress we have made, the present levels of human distress and wasted effort are still too high to bear.

The solution of a problem – any problem – consists in discovering how to transform an existing state of affairs into a desired one that has not yet come into being. Now in order to do this effectively one clearly needs not only a good idea of the desired end state but a good understanding of the features of the starting point. Thus teachers need to be clear not only about what they would like children to become under their guidance but about what children are actually like when the process is begun.

During the past few years, research has yielded much new

evidence about the basic skills of thought and language which children already possess when they come to school. It is time for us to reconsider some widely held beliefs, and to ask what the revision of them implies.

2. The Ability to 'Decentre'

I spent that first day picking holes in paper, then went home in a smouldering temper.

'What's the matter, Love? Didn't he like it at school, then?'

'They never gave me the present.'

'Present? What present?'

'They said they'd give me a present.'

'Well, now, I'm sure they didn't.'

'They did! They said: "You're Laurie Lee, aren't you? Well just you sit there for the present." I sat there all day but I never got it. I ain't going back there again.'

(Laurie Lee)

We laugh at this misunderstanding for at least two reasons: because of the shock that comes from the sudden recognition of ambiguity where normally we would see none; and because the child's interpretation touches us by revealing the inadequacy of his expectations, the naïveté of his open and hopeful mind.

The obvious first way to look at this episode is to say that the child did not understand the adult. Yet it is clear on a very little reflection that the adult also failed, at a deeper level, in understanding the child – in placing himself imaginatively at the child's point of view.

This is not to criticize the teacher who spoke these words to Laurie Lee. We cannot stop to reflect on every word we utter as we hurry through a day.

Nevertheless this teacher was behaving, however

understandably, in a way that psychologists would call 'ego-centric'. Used in this way, the word does not mean 'selfish', but it does mean, in a precise sense, 'self-centred'. It refers to the act of looking out on the world from one's own position in it, literally or metaphorically, and failing to realize how the same world, seen from a different stance, would appear – or what meaning the same words, heard and interpreted by a different brain with a different store of previous knowledge and experience, would carry.

Laurie Lee did not know that school is not a place where one normally gets presents. The teacher did know this, and she forgot that he did not. She knew it so well that it probably never entered her head that anyone else might fail to know it. The better you know something, the more risk there is of behaving egocentrically in relation to your knowledge. Thus the greater the gap between teacher and learner the harder teaching becomes, in this respect at least.

Also, Laurie Lee probably had no knowledge at all of the other, idiomatic, adult meaning of the words 'for the present'. So he did not even have an alternative interpretation to con-sider. In this respect too the teacher forgot about the size of the gap between them. She acted from her own self-centre. She failed to 'decentre' and consider imaginatively what her words would be likely to mean to a small child.

We all have a very strong tendency to 'act from the centre' in this sort of way. Yet we are highly skilled at decentring also, otherwise communication would fail completely much more often than it does. If there were someone who was quite unable to take account of the point of view of another person, then he would be a very poor communicator. For a conversa-tion to go smoothly, each participant needs to try to under-stand what the other knows already, does not know, needs to know for his purposes, wants to know for his pleasure.

It has been claimed that children under the age of six or seven are very bad at communicating, precisely for the reason that they are bad at decentring – or that they are highly 'egocentric'.

This claim has been made most forcibly by Jean Piaget, and it has been backed by much supporting evidence. He has made it central to his theorizing about the capacities of children in

18

the pre-school and early school years. He has constructed such a far-reaching and closely woven net of argument, binding together so many different features of the development of behaviour, that it is hard to believe he could be wrong.

Yet there is now powerful evidence that in this respect he *is* wrong.

In recent years Piaget has collected most of his data by devising tasks for children to do and then observing their behaviour when they deal with the task, questioning them about it, noting what they say. One of the best known of these tasks is concerned with the ability to take account of someone else's point of view in the literal sense – that is, to recognize what someone else will see who is looking at the same thing as oneself but from the other side.

For this task, a three-dimensional object or set of objects is needed. Piaget uses a model of three mountains. (See *The Child's Conception of Space* by Piaget and Inhelder.) The mountains are distinguished from one another by colour and by such features as snow on one, a house on top of another, a red cross at the summit of the third.

The child sits at one side of the table on which this model is placed. The experimenter then produces a little doll and puts the doll at some other position round the table. The problem for the child is: what does the doll see?

It would clearly be hard for the child to give a verbal description ('He sees a house on top of the mountain on his right . . .' etc.) for that description would have to be of considerable complexity. So in one version of the task the child is given a set of ten pictures of the model taken from different angles, and he is asked to choose the one which shows what the doll sees. In another version he is given three cardboard 'mountains' and he is asked to arrange them so that they represent what would be seen in a snapshot taken from the doll's position. Children up to the age of around eight, or even nine, cannot as a rule do this successfully; and there is a powerful tendency among children below the age of six or seven to choose the picture – or build the model – which represents their own point of view – exactly what they themselves see.

Piaget takes this to indicate that they are unable to 'de-centre' in imagination. He points out that in one sense they know perfectly well that the appearance of a thing changes when you walk round it. And yet he maintains that they are bound by what he calls 'the egocentric illusion' as soon as they are called upon to form a mental representation of some view which they have not actually seen. They 'really imagine that the doll's perspective is the same as their own' (p. 220). They all think the doll sees the mountains only as they look from the child's position. What the child lacks is held to be the ability to see his own momentary viewpoint as one of a set of possible viewpoints, and to co-ordinate these possibilities into a single coherent system, so that he understands the ways in which the different perspectives relate to one another.

We are urged by Piaget to believe that the child's behaviour in this situation gives us a deep insight into the nature of his world. This world is held to be one that is composed largely of 'false absolutes'. That is to say, the child does not appreciate that what he sees is relative to his own position; he takes it to represent absolute truth or reality – *the world as it really is*. Notice that this implies a world marked by extreme discontinuity. Any change in position means abrupt change in the world and a sharp break with the past. And indeed Piaget believes that this is how it is for the young child: that he lives in the state of the moment, not bothering himself with how things were just previously, with the relation of one state to those which come before or after it. His world is like a film run slowly, as Piaget says elsewhere.

This is by no means to say that Piaget thinks the child has no memory of the earlier 'stills'. The issue for Piaget is how the momentary states are linked, or fail to be linked, in the child's mind. The issue is how well the child can deal conceptually with the transitions between them.

All this has far-reaching implications for the child's ability to think and reason, and we shall come back to these implications later. But first let us consider how children perform on a task which is in some ways very like the 'mountains' task and in other extremely important ways very different.

This task was devised by Martin Hughes. In its simplest form, it makes use of two 'walls' intersecting to form a cross, and two small dolls, representing respectively a policeman and a little boy. Seen from above, the lay-out (before the boy doll is put in position) is like this:

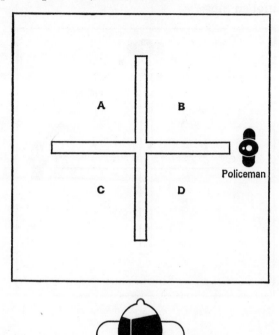

In the studies which Hughes conducted the policeman was placed initially as in the diagram so that he could see the areas marked B and D, while the areas A and C were hidden from him by the wall.

The child was then introduced to the task very carefully, in ways that were designed to give him every chance of understanding the situation fully and grasping what was being asked of him. First, Hughes put the boy doll in section A and asked if the policeman could see the boy there. The question was repeated for sections B, C and D in turn. Next the policeman was placed on the opposite side, facing the wall that divides A from C, and the child was asked to 'hide the doll so that the policeman can't see him'. If the child made any mistakes at these preliminary stages, his error was pointed out to him, and the question was repeated until the correct answer was given.

But very few mistakes were made.

Then the test proper began. And now the task was made more complex. Another policeman was produced and the two were positioned thus:

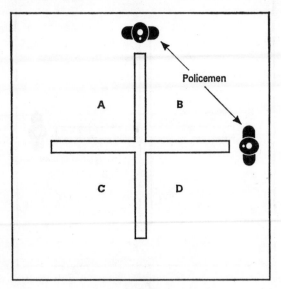

Child

The child was told to hide the boy from both policemen, a result which could only be achieved by the consideration and co-ordination of two different points of view. This was repeated three times, so that each time a different section was left as the only hiding place.

The results were dramatic. When thirty children between the ages of three-and-a-half and five years were given this task, 90 per cent of their responses were correct. And even the ten youngest children, whose average age was only three years nine months, achieved a success rate of 88 per cent.

Hughes then went on to further trials, using more complex arrangements of walls, with as many as five or six sections, and introducing a third policeman. The three-year-olds had more trouble with this, but they still got over 60 per cent of the trials correct. The four-year-olds could still succeed at the 90-per-cent level.

It seems to be impossible to reconcile these findings with Piaget's claim that children under the age of seven are very bad at appreciating the point of view of some other person in the literal sense of being unable to figure out what that other person can see. However, though Hughes' findings cannot be reconciled with Piaget's *claim*, some way must be found of reconciling them with Piaget's *findings* – for these are not suspect. Research by other investigators has fully confirmed that, if children are given the Piaget 'mountains' task, they do indeed have extreme difficulty with it – but not, it now seems, for the reason Piaget suggests. For what reason, then?

One must obviously consider the differences between the two tasks – and these are many. One difference which Hughes noted is that the 'policemen' task, while it certainly involves the co-ordination of points of view, merely requires the child to figure out whether an object will be visible and does not require him to deal with left–right reversals and so on. That is, he must decide *what* can be seen but not exactly *how* it will appear. Now it is perfectly clear that the calculation of how something will look from a given position when the scene is fairly complex will give pause to many an adult. But this hardly seems to explain why young children, in tackling the 'mountains' task, so frequently choose their own point of view instead of a different, though wrong, one. When this fact is considered along with Hughes' findings, it is difficult to avoid the conclusion that the children who make 'egocentric' responses to the 'mountains' problem do not fully understand what they are supposed to do.*

By contrast it is quite evident that, in the 'policemen' problem, a situation has been found which *makes sense* to the child. Hughes was very careful about introducing the tasks in

* In another study, Hughes used a simplified version of the mountains task and found that it was possible, by taking great care over the way in which the problem was introduced, to get a high proportion of correct responses from pre-school children. So this lends further support to the view that Piaget's subjects did not understand.

ways that would help the children to understand the nature of the problem, but in fact his precautions were largely unnecessary: the children seemed to grasp the situation at once. We have then to ask why this was so easy for them.

Notice that we cannot appeal to direct actual experience: few, if any, of these children had ever tried to hide from a policeman. But we *can* appeal to the generalization of experience: they know what it is to try to hide. Also they know what it is to be naughty and to want to evade the consequences. So they can easily conceive that a boy might want to hide from a policeman if he had been a bad boy; for in this case it would be the job of the policeman to catch him and the consequences of being caught would be undesirable.

The point is that the *motives* and *intentions* of the characters are entirely comprehensible, even to a child of three. The task requires the child to act in ways which are in line with certain very basic human purposes and interactions (escape and pursuit) – it makes *human sense*. Thus it is not at all hard to convey to the child what he is supposed to do: he apprehends it instantly. It then turns out that neither is it hard for him to do it. In other words, in this context he shows none of the difficulty in 'decentring' which Piaget ascribes to him.

In respect of being humanly comprehensible, the 'mountains' task is at the opposite extreme. Within this task itself, there is no play of interpersonal motives of such a kind as to make it instantly intelligible. (There is the question of the experimenter's motives in asking the child to do it and of the child's motives in responding, but that is quite another matter.)

Thus the 'mountains' task is *abstract* in a psychologically very important sense: in the sense that it is abstracted from all basic human purposes and feelings and endeavours. It is totally cold-blooded. In the veins of three-year-olds, the blood still runs warm.

This is in no way meant to suggest that the ability to deal, in cold blood, with problems of an abstract and formal nature is unimportant. It is immensely important. Much that is distinctively human and highly to be valued depends upon it. And young children are bad at it.

The more highly one values this activity the more important

it then becomes to try to understand the true nature of the difficulty to which it gives rise. For the better we understand this, the more readily we should be able to help children to overcome it.

One obstacle that stands in the way of better understanding is that those who study such topics are, for the most part, accustomed to abstract and formal modes of thought to the point where they find it hard to appreciate that degrees of abstractness which present no kind of difficulty to them may render a task senseless and bewildering to a child. In other words, the research worker, like Laurie Lee's teacher, may often fail to decentre.

It may seem now that we have reached the curious position of claiming (a) that children are not egocentric, and (b) that sophisticated adults are. Not so, however. What is being claimed is that we are all egocentric through the whole of our lives in some situations and very well able to decentre in others. Piaget would not disagree with the claim that egocentrism is never wholly overcome. The dispute with him is only about the extent – and the developmental significance – of egocentrism in early childhood. I want to argue that the difference between child and adult in this respect is less than he supposes; and then to argue further that the critical differences lie elsewhere.

In the course of trying to reconcile Hughes' findings with Piaget's I suggested that Hughes' task is easy for the child to grasp because it makes human sense. It rests on an understanding of the interaction of two complementary intentions of a very basic kind: the intention to escape and the intention to pursue and capture. Now it is worth observing that the appreciation of such a complementary pair of intentions, however simple and elementary, calls already for an ability to decentre that is not concerned with the literal understanding of another point of view: not with what another person *sees* from a given standpoint, but with what he is feeling or planning to do. Hughes' task, though designed primarily to test the former, also rests upon the latter. And what I have been suggesting is that the latter is a very fundamental human skill.

The question of the origins of this skill takes us right back to infancy, at which time Piaget believes that the most profound egocentrism reigns. He holds that initially the child is not capable of making any distinction between himself and what is not himself, that he cannot draw the boundary which later, most of the time, is so obvious and so firm.

This is a degree or two more extreme than simply attributing to the rest of existence your own point of view; for if you deny existence to the rest of existence you evidently deny it any point of view at all. But by the same token you deny it to yourself. The whole notion of 'point of view' ceases to apply.

Piaget calls this early egocentrism 'complete *and unconscious*' (my italics). If the child is in this state then he is not aware of himself, any more than he is aware of other people and things. Awareness grows as differentiation grows.

It is quite reasonable to wonder how Piaget or anyone else knows what a very young infant is aware of. Certainly the infant cannot tell us directly. So the only possibility is to try to make inferences from the way he behaves.

The central piece of evidence from which Piaget argues is this: if you let a child of five or six months play with a small toy and you then cover that toy with a box or a cloth while the child is watching you, the child will most commonly make no attempt to lift the cover and get at the toy again. This will be true even if the child has shown much interest in the toy and even if you know from other evidence that his control of hand and arm movements is quite good enough for him to manage the reaching and grasping that would be needed.

So why does he not do his best to get the toy back again? Piaget argues that he does not do this for the interesting reason that the toy has ceased to exist for him: at this stage out of sight really *is* out of mind.

An adult normally thinks of the world as a place where objects endure in their own right, whether or not he sees them. Their existence is independent of his. Some philosophers have questioned this notion and its bases, but for most of us, most of the time, it is a quite unchallenged assumption, continually guiding our behaviour. If we see a box being placed over an object, we know that the object is still there. If someone were to take away the box and show us that the object had vanished, we would be considerably surprised and we would have to invoke trickery or magic.

So if a child does not believe that the object is still there inside the box, if he has not developed what has come to be called the 'object concept', then his notion of the world must be very different from our own. But so it would be if he had not distinguished himself from the rest of the universe. You cannot think of a universe of stable enduring things, moving around in space and time, unless you have made the critical distinction between self and not-self by which you award the things their independence – and at the same time achieve your own.

Thus Piaget uses the child's failure to search for a vanished object as evidence for a state of profound early egocentrism. And at first sight it seems like strong evidence indeed. But there are various difficulties for his conclusion, and a substantial one is this: if the reason why the child does not search is because he totally lacks the concept of the permanence of objects, then the precise way in which an object is made to vanish from his sight should not make any difference to his response. If the world for him is just a series of pictures that come and go (which is what the lack of the object concept would seem to imply), then, no matter what causes the object to vanish, the child will still not try to get it back. However, this does not appear to be true. The manner of disappearance does matter.

One way of causing an object to disappear from human eyes is to remove all light from it. And it is possible with modern infra-red television cameras to photograph events that occur in total darkness. So an object can be made to vanish simply by switching off the lights in a blacked-out room, and the child's behaviour can then still be observed. This experiment has been carried out by Tom Bower and Jennifer Wishart, and they report that in these circumstances children quickly reach out in the appropriate direction to find their toy again. Thus Piaget's claims about egocentrism are once again challenged.

In this instance, there is still a good deal of debate about what the right explanation will finally prove to be, and there is much ongoing research. But Bower offers an interesting and well-supported account which proposes that it is with the notions of location and movement that the child's initial difficulties lie. (See *A Primer of Infant Development*.) On this view of the matter, what the young infant lacks is the knowledge that objects *move* and that this fact makes it possible for the same object to appear in different places or for different objects to appear in the same place, either one after the other or one inside the other. But by the age of five months, some notion of movement is present and the understanding that object X can go from place A to place B is established. Thereafter the child continues to have many difficulties of the kind Piaget describes, but they arise from the fact that he has yet to develop a full appreciation of spatial relations such as *on*, *in*, *in front of*, and *behind*.* They do not derive from the complete lack of a notion of a world of 'other things'.

Among the 'other things' in the universe, there is one group specially important for a human baby, whether or not he is aware of the fact, and that is the group of other persons. Now one consequence of a belief in profound early egocentrism has to be the belief that the baby is quite unaware of the special significance of other people. And he certainly must be incapable of genuinely social behaviour – incapable of any response to persons as persons, of any communication with them, of any apprehension of their intentions. The overwhelming impression which the adult gets of being in touch, humanly speaking, with the baby must be illusory.

Piaget goes so far as to allow that, by seven or eight months, the child does show by the very look on his face that people keenly interest him. But to be consistent Piaget must go on, as indeed he does go on, to say that in the child's mind there is still no contrast in principle between another person and the rest of the universe. (See *The Child's Construction of Reality*.)

If, on the other hand, we do not accept that the baby is wholly bound in egocentrism, we are free to allow that his interest in other people is as genuine as it appears to be, and that some kinds of personal interaction are at least possible at an early stage: that some sort of genuine two-way communica-

---

* We are not talking here about the understanding of these *words*, but of the relationships to which they refer.

tion may be going on. But is it? There is a certain risk here of believing something because we want to believe it. It is emotionally more satisfying for most adults to think that the young baby who smiles at them is already a person than to think that the smiles and gestures and vocalizings are largely reflexive, that they are merely blind behaviour patterns devoid of personal meaning. So there is need for caution. Yet many workers who have closely observed the interactions of mothers and young babies are now convinced that the impression of personal response from a baby is by no means illusory and that communicative strivings begin within the first few months of life. Thus Jerome Bruner presents evidence which supports the view that adult and infant can very soon come to a sharing of attention and a communication of intention, and he takes this early 'mutuality' to be the essential starting point for the learning of language. (See 'The ontogenesis of speech acts'.) Kindred findings and arguments come from Colwyn Trevarthen who claims that evidence from films of more than 100 exchanges between mothers and their infants of two or three months of age forces us to conclude that a complex form of mutual understanding develops even at this age. Trevarthen believes that this kind of early interpersonal responsiveness is the source from which the whole of human intelligence springs.

Certainly, once the child begins to speak, the existence of communicative strivings cannot be doubted; and it would appear to ordinary observation as if the capacity for mutual exchange develops very rapidly thereafter. Yet even here the question of egocentrism arises.

It was indeed in the course of discussing his observations of the speech of pre-school children that Piaget first proposed egocentrism as an explanatory concept, claiming that much of the time when the young child speaks he 'does not attempt to place himself at the point of view of his hearer'. (See *The Language and Thought of the Child*.)

Once again, however, later work has made it necessary to call in question not the claim that the child sometimes fails to do this, but certainly any suggestion that he cannot. Michael Maratsos reports a study in which young children were asked to communicate about a set of toys to an adult who was either herself looking at the toys or who had closed her eyes and covered them with her hand. (Actually she was cheating by peeping through!) The task for the child was to let the adult know which toy was to be put in a car that was then to be run down a hill; and sometimes – for instance, when there were two identical objects in different positions – this put a considerable strain on the children's linguistic resources. It was not easy for them to produce descriptions like: 'the one that is nearest to the car'. So, very reasonably, when the adult could see, the children for the most part dealt with such problems simply by pointing. But when they believed she could not see, they tried to give verbal descriptions even though they could not manage these well. As Maratsos puts it, they showed high sensitivity to the listener's state. Maratsos explains the fact that some other investigators have not reported so much sensitivity of this kind in young children by pointing out that he himself used a very simple task – one which the children could readily understand.

Peter Lloyd, in a study that raised the same kind of issue, used a task involving a talking toy panda, presented to the children as a creature who 'could not speak very well' and who would therefore need their help when he tried to communicate. (The panda's voice actually came from an adult hidden in a sound-proof cubicle with a one-way vision screen.) The children gave help with obvious pleasure and most of them showed themselves to be sensitive to the panda's incompetence, making allowance for it in their dealings with him.

Lloyd found that, though the children would try to help the panda, they were not so ready to signal when they themselves needed help. They were not given to indicating that a message which they had received was inadequate. They did not often spontaneously ask for more information. But many of them proved to be able to do this quite competently if they were explicitly encouraged to tell the panda whenever he did not say enough. All in all, there was little indication of the existence of egocentrism as a serious barrier to communication.

The general conclusion seems unavoidable: pre-school children are not nearly so limited in their ability to 'decentre', or appreciate someone else's point of view, as Piaget has for many years maintained.

The abandonment of belief in pronounced childhood ego-centrism has far-reaching implications. But its significance will be better understood if it is seen in the light of recent evidence and arguments about the ways in which children learn to use and understand language. So it is to a consideration of this that we now turn.

3. Learning Language

It has become fashionable recently to talk, not of *learning* to speak, but of *acquiring* language. This is the result of a kind of revolution which took place in the 1960s and which was due to the work of the American linguist, Noam Chomsky.

As regards the growth of a child's knowledge of his language, Chomsky's central thesis was – and is – that we are innately equipped with knowledge about what human language is like – about the *kind* of system it is. He supposes us to be provided from birth with a special sensitivity to those features of the grammars of human language which are 'universal' – that is, not specific to any given tongue. Thus we are able quickly to recognize, or 'latch on' to, the ways in which these features manifest themselves in the particular human language with which we happen to be dealing – Chinese or Finnish or Hebrew or whatever, as the case may be.

Notice, first of all, that in this account the stress is on *grammar*. The emphasis is on how the child comes by his knowledge of the structure of the language, of the rules which control the ways in which words may be combined with other words to form acceptable utterances.

This was a topic which had previously received very little attention from students of child language, and Chomsky's work generated a sudden rush of interest in the problem – an interest so great that, for a while, almost every other aspect of language learning was ignored. The research to which this interest gave rise seemed at first to confirm the claim that children had mastered the grammar of their language at a very early age. And this mastery appeared to involve the child in really formulating the rules for himself. Much was made of the fact that children's errors were sometimes 'rule-revealing'. It was argued that a child who says 'I bringed it' must have formulated (in some sense, though presumably not consciously) the rule that you make the past tense of a verb by adding –ed to the present tense. The error would then arise simply because he applied the rule too widely, not yet having come to know the exceptions. At any rate it was clear that he had not learned 'I bringed it' by direct imitation of adults, for this is not an error that they are at all likely to make.

What was specially exciting against this background was the finding that children will sometimes begin by saying 'I brought' correctly and then for a time abandon the correct form in favour of the erroneous one. This made it seem clear that the child's active building of his own grammar was a process which could over-ride other kinds of learning; and students of child language spent a great deal of time trying to specify the grammar which a child was using at any given stage in his development. They did this by collecting a 'corpus' of as many as possible of the things the child had said, and then trying to work out a set of rules by which just these utterances might have been generated.

Little attention was paid, at the height of this activity, to the question of what the child might mean by the things he was saying, and still less to the question of his ability to understand the words of others. It was widely accepted, however, that his understanding would be generally in advance of his ability to speak. 'Comprehension precedes production' was the dictum. This seemed like common sense and such research as had been done appeared on the whole to support it. (But see the discussion in Chapter 6, pages 72–5.)

In order to understand how significant the work on child grammar appeared a decade ago, it is necessary to think of it in relation to the ideas that were then dominant concerning other aspects of the development of the mind. In particular, the work on child language has to be seen in relation to the work of Piaget, and to Piaget's claim that the child under the age of seven is in many ways extremely limited in his ability to think and reason. We have already seen that the Piagetian pre-school child is not supposed to know what an object would look like from the other side. To give some further examples of his limitations, he is supposed to think that if you pour water from a jar into another jar of a different shape you change the amount of the water. Further, he is not supposed to realize that if a red stick is longer than a yellow stick, and if that yellow stick is longer than a blue stick, then the red stick must be longer than the blue stick; and so on.

By the mid-1960s, a flood of researches had been pouring out of Geneva for years, all of them tending to the same conclusion: the child under seven is very restricted intellectually. He has developed considerable skills on a practical level, mastering these rapidly during the first eighteen months of his life. But he is not much of a thinker.

During the 1960s this work by Piaget and his colleagues was at the peak of its influence. It was very widely known and very widely accepted.

Against this background the claims about the child as a grammarian were dramatic. How was one to explain that a child who, on the one hand, was baffled by many things which seemed utterly simple and obvious to an adult could, on the other hand, work out for himself the rules of such a highly complex system as a human language?

To this question Chomsky proposed an answer: the child must have a *highly specific* predisposition to understand this kind of system. He must be born with a 'language acquisition device'.*

The language acquisition device, or LAD as it was called, was pictured as a kind of box. Into this 'box' (which was presumably located somewhere in the central nervous system,

* I do not intend to imply that Chomsky himself was directly influenced by Piaget's work when he postulated the language acquisition device. But I think that, for many psychologists, Chomsky's claims were rendered more striking and interesting by being considered in the context of Piagetian findings. On the other hand, Piagetian theory conflicts in many ways with the Chomskyan position. It would take a whole book to do justice to the relations between the two.

though not literally as a box, of course) there went, via the child's ears, linguistic input – input that was often very scrappy, fragments of the discourse that the child was hearing around him. But the device was so well tuned to the key features of human language that from this inadequate input it could extract the rules of the grammar – so sensitive and well prepared that it could produce almost immediately the right hypotheses about what these rules might be.

It proved to be an extraordinarily compelling idea. Almost everyone in the affected disciplines succumbed at least for a time to its seductive power. One of its consequences was to set human beings very firmly apart from the other mammals, who evidently lacked such a device. It was of course no new idea that man is set apart by his language-learning skills. But this notion of the special human LAD provided a new kind of focus for the old apartheid.*

In 1965 Chomsky stated his position like this:

> It seems plain that language acquisition is based on the child's discovery of what from a formal point of view is *a deep and abstract theory* – a generative grammar of his language – many of the concepts and principles of which are *only remotely related to experience* by long and intricate chains of unconscious quasi-inferential steps. [My italics]

Before Chomsky, the closeness to experience of the language-learning process had been the main emphasis. This emphasis is now returning, but in a very different form.

In the 1930s, 1940s and 1950s there was a conception of how language was learned which in its broad outlines went almost unchallenged at that time. Many variant theories existed, but the basic notion was that a word acquired its meaning by occurring *together with* the thing which it meant or *stood for*. Language was conceived as a vast network of

---

* Yet in June 1966 two American psychologists, Allen and Beatrice Gardner, were already undertaking the apparently hopeless task of teaching American Sign Language to Washoe, a chimpanzee – a task which turned out not to be so hopeless after all.

associative links between separate elements: individual words and individual 'things'. Thus a child's language-learning history was the history of the formation and strengthening of these bonds. And sometimes the following sort of account was offered to explain how the process got begun.

While a mother is looking after her baby she normally makes human speech sounds. The child has a natural tendency to vocalize randomly himself. Some of his sounds will come close to those his mother makes and will thus be associated with the relief and satisfaction which her presence and her care bring to him. He will then tend more and more to make those sounds rather than others in his repertoire – and gradually he will discover that these sounds not only satisfy him, but produce desirable responses from his parents. Thus he will begin to *use* them.

There is no point now in discussing how, starting from one or other version of the 'associationist' position, psychologists tried to explain the full development of language in all its richness and flexibility. The attempts were sometimes ingenious. They achieved some partial successes that looked promising. In the end they all failed.

The Chomskyan revolution was a revolt against them; and Chomsky's attack on the significance of experience was the flag to which the rebels rallied. A child with a language acquisition device had need of experience indeed, but only to set going processes which were destined to depend upon it very little thereafter.

Now in the 1970s another revolt has begun. It is milder, and it lacks one powerfully dominant leader. But it is gathering strength.

In 1972 John Macnamara wrote a paper which stands Chomsky's argument about the language acquisition device upon its head. In place of the claim that children have an 'acquisition device' whose content is highly specific to language, with the result that language acquisition shoots ahead of the other skills of the mind, Macnamara proposed that children are able to learn language precisely because they possess certain other skills – and specifically because they have a relatively well-developed capacity for making sense of certain types of situation involving direct and immediate human interaction.

To understand how this might work, imagine, for instance, the following scene. An English woman is in the company of an Arab woman and her two children, a boy of seven and a little girl of thirteen months who is just beginning to walk but is afraid to take more than a few steps without help. The English woman speaks no Arabic, the Arab woman and her son speak no English.

The little girl walks to the English woman and back to her mother. Then she turns as if to start off in the direction of the English woman once again. But the latter now smiles, points to the boy and says: 'Walk to your brother this time.' At once the boy, *understanding the situation* though he understands not a word of the language, holds out his arms. The baby smiles, changes direction and walks to her brother. Like the older child, she appears to have understood the situation perfectly.

These events occurred as I have described them. The thing to notice is that the words 'Walk to your brother this time' were such as to fit with complete appropriateness the patterns of interaction. All the participants understood the situation in the sense that they understood one another's intentions. The language was unnecessary but it was uttered – and its meaning was highly predictable in the human context of its occurrence. What the people meant was clear. What the words meant could in principle be derived from that.

It is evident that some kind of association is involved here – and is indeed essential to this account of what is going on. It is possible to figure out what the words mean because they occur *together with* certain non-linguistic events. But beyond this all likeness to the old associationist accounts disappears. The whole nature of the explanation is different, for it implies a totally different conception of the nature of the human mind.

The old idea was that the associations were built up in quite mechanical automatic ways. They were bonds between isolated elements. The person in whom these bonds developed was passive. Something happened to him, and an association between, say, a word and a thing was the result. The associations came first. Insofar as there was 'meaning' it was an outcome of the (conditioning) process by which the

37

associations were established.

The newer account differs from this in the most fundamental way. The primary thing is now held to be the grasp of meaning – the ability to 'make sense' of things, and above all to make sense of what people do, which of course includes what people say. On this view, it is the child's ability to interpret situations which makes it possible for him, through active processes of hypothesis-testing and inference, to arrive at a knowledge of language.

Now there is an important condition which must be satisfied if this account is to hold: the child must be in a general way capable of inference. For it is no longer being claimed that when he learns language he is using skills highly specific to that task. On the contrary, language learning is now presented as being closely bound up with all the other learning that is going on.

Indeed for a long time the learning of language may be bound up with non-linguistic concerns more inextricably than has appeared in anything that has been said so far. It may turn out to be a very long journey from the primary understanding of what people mean by the words they speak and by their concomitant acts to the ultimate and separate understanding of what *words* mean. Perhaps the idea that words mean anything – in isolation – is a highly sophisticated adult notion, and a Western adult notion at that.

Heinz Werner tells the story of an explorer who was interested in the language of a North American Indian tribe and who asked a native speaker to translate into his language the sentence: 'The white man shot six bears today.' The Indian said it was impossible. The explorer was puzzled, and asked him to explain. 'How can I do that?' said the Indian. 'No white man could shoot six bears in one day.'

To Western adults, and especially to Western adult linguists, languages are formal systems. A formal system can be manipulated in a formal way. It is an easy but dangerous move from this to the conclusion that it is also learned in a formal way.

Chomsky's LAD is a formal data processor, in its way just as automatic and mechanical as processes of an associationist kind. In go the linguistic data, out comes a grammar. The living child does not seem to enter into the business very actively (not to say fully) in either case. What does the warm blood in the veins matter? It actually figures more in some associationist accounts than in the Chomskyan one.

4. Failing to Reason or Failing to Understand?

The term 'deductive inference' is apt to suggest something daunting. But basically, deductive inference is very simple indeed. It is the drawing of the conclusion that if something is true, something else must also be true.

Here is an example. If the number of sweets in a red box is greater than the number in a green box; and if the number in the green box is greater than the number in a blue box; then the number in the red box is greater than the number in the blue box. This conclusion is self-evident to any normal adult.

We can state the essence of the thing in a number of ways. The truth of the first two statements – the premises – makes the truth of the third statement – the conclusion – *necessary*. If the first two are true, then nothing else is *possible* than that the third is true also. The truth of the first two statements is not *compatible* with the falsehood of the third.

The key notions are compatibility, possibility and necessity. No one who totally lacked a sense of these could make deductive inferences. (It is not of course at all necessary to know these words or to have reflected upon these ideas.)

The notions of compatibility, possibility and necessity are very closely connected with one another but perhaps there is a case for saying that compatibility is the most fundamental. Having a sense of compatibility and incompatibility amounts to understanding that we live in a world where the existence of one state of affairs may sometimes rule out the existence of another. This is so fundamental that it is impossible to imagine a 'real world' where it would not be true. If an object is a tree it cannot also be an aeroplane; if it is a circle it cannot also be a square; if it is bigger than another object it cannot at the same time be smaller than that same object.

As soon as language is used to describe the world, even in a rudimentary fashion, then questions of compatibility arise. The use of any form of language to make descriptive statements must rest on some recognition that certain states of affairs cannot exist together. As soon as a child identifies an object as a dog by saying 'That bow-wow' his statement is incompatible with an infinite number of others that could be made. To assert is also to deny. And if the child did not in some sense recognize this he could not make meaningful utterances at all, or understand what other people mean when they speak to him. On the other hand the statement, 'That bow-wow' is evidently *compatible* with many others – e.g. 'That's brown'; 'That's big'; 'That's a spaniel'. The child needs to learn which statements are compatible with one another and which are not.

It seems likely that the earliest recognition of what an utterance *excludes* may be very dim indeed. And it may be some time before the fundamental sense that certain things cannot occur together is used as a way of extending knowledge. For that, in practice, is the usefulness of deductive inference. It means that there are some things which we can know without checking upon them directly. Given certain information, we can be sure of other things about which we have no direct evidence – things perhaps which we are in no position to verify, but on which we can nevertheless rely. For a creature that has to cope with a complex world, this is obviously a very valuable skill. And the growth of this skill is of very great interest to anyone who is concerned to understand the growth of the mind.

To say that some sense of compatibility and incompatibility is essential for deductive inference is not, of course, to say that this is all that is required. Piaget considers that the growth of the ability to decentre is crucial. His argument is that the making of inferences demands skill in the flexible shifting of point of view.

To illustrate what he means, let us take a task which he has devised and which bears on a matter with which logicians have traditionally been much concerned: the relation of a class of objects to its sub-classes. Any class can in principle be divided up into sub-classes in a variety of ways. For instance, the class of toys can be divided into those which represent animals, like teddy bears, and those which do not. Given such sub-divisions, various simple inferences are possible, such as that all toy animals are toys, that some (but not all) toys are toy animals and so on. The fundamental inference, however, is that, if there are two or more sub-classes each of which contains at least one member, then the number of objects in the total class has to be greater than the number in any sub-class: the number of toys must be greater than the number of toy animals.

All of this seems self-evident, as is the way with certain elementary inferences. Is it so to a child? Piaget claims that before the age of six or seven it is not self-evident at all, and he supports his claim in the following way.

The child is shown a number of objects of some familiar kind – say, a bunch of flowers, or a number of beads. Whatever the objects chosen, they must divide into two sub-classes in some fairly obvious manner: some of the flowers must be red, some white, some of the beads must be wooden, some plastic, and so on. Also the numbers in the two sub-classes should, for the normal version of the task, be unequal. (See *The Child's Conception of Number* (by Piaget) and *The Early Growth of Logic in the Child* (by Inhelder and Piaget).)

Suppose that there are in fact four red flowers and two white flowers. The question for the child to answer is then: Are there more red flowers or more flowers? And the usual answer from a child of, say, five is that there are more red flowers.

This finding has provoked a great deal of controversy, and much research beyond that which initially produced it. The first thing to look at, however, is Piaget's own explanation.

He points out that if you ask a child who has given this answer what would be left if you took away the red flowers, he will promptly tell you 'the white flowers'; and if you ask him what would be left if you took away all the flowers he will tell you 'nothing'. So it looks as if he knows what these terms mean, and as if he knows in some sense that the total set is more numerous than the sub-set. But this second form of question allows him to think successively of the whole class (the flowers) and the sub-classes (the red and the white). The other form of questioning (Are there more flowers or more red flowers?) requires him to think of them simultaneously. Now Piaget's claim is that, if the child *centres* on the whole class, he cannot at the same time think of the parts which compose it. Thus the seemingly simple comparison of whole with part is impossible. He lacks the particular sort of mental flexibility which this demands. His thinking is still a succession of separate views of things, poorly co-ordinated with one another (cf. page 20). So he cannot reason as to the relations between them.

The deficiency is held to be general. The young child's response to the 'class-inclusion' task is seen as just one manifestation of an extremely important and widespread limitation which is usually overcome around the age of seven when, in Piagetian terminology, the thinking of the child becomes 'operational'. ('Operational', as used by Piaget, is a technical term. See Appendix.)

We have already seen that there is good reason to doubt whether the child's difficulty with decentring is as severe and widespread as Piaget claims. However, none of the research we have so far discussed deals explicitly with any task which Piaget takes to be criterial for the appearance of operational thought. It would be entirely possible for difficulties with decentration to occur when the child is presented with a task like class inclusion, even if they do not arise in certain other contexts. So, direct study of these tasks is necessary. A very enlightening set of experiments was designed and carried out by James McGarrigle a few years ago, to see if the Piagetian explanation would really stand up to rigorous scrutiny.

There is not much doubt about what a child *does* when he makes the standard type of error and says there are more red flowers than flowers: he compares one sub-class with the other sub-class. His spontaneous remarks often make this quite clear. He will say: 'More red flowers because there are only two white ones' and so on. The question is why does he compare sub-class with sub-class? Is it because he *cannot* compare sub-class with class, as Piaget maintains? Or is it because he thinks this is what he is meant to do?* Is there once more *a failure of communication*?

If the latter explanation is correct it ought to be possible to find different ways of presenting the problem which will make it easier or harder; and one should be able to discover just what it is that makes the child misinterpret the question that is asked of him.

Notice that even an adult may well misinterpret this question initially; but repetition of the question, perhaps with added stress on the word *flowers*, will quickly enable him to get it right. This is not normally enough to make a young child change his mind, but it does suggest the idea that the giving of some greater emphasis to the total class might be effective; and so might the reduction of emphasis on the contrast between the sub-classes.

McGarrigle tried ways of achieving both of these effects. In relation to the first he used four toy cows, three of them black, one of them white. He laid all the cows on their sides and he explained that they were 'sleeping'. The experiment then rested on comparison of the difficulty of two different forms of question:

1 Are there more black cows or more cows? (the standard Piagetian form); and

2 Are there more black cows or more sleeping cows?

For both of these questions the cows were in fact laid on their sides: the situations were identical except for the wording of the question. McGarrigle's argument was that the introduction of the adjective 'sleeping' would increase the emphasis on the total class.

The average age of the children was six years. Question 1 was answered correctly by 25 per cent of the group (12 children); question 2 was answered correctly by 48 per cent

---

* There is also the possibility that he knows what he is meant to do, is capable of doing it, but chooses not to, because he is unwilling to play the experimenter's game. This might happen occasionally. But few children give any sign of being perverse in this way. The amazing thing is how willing they usually are to try to do anything that is asked of them.

(23 children). The difference was statistically significant – there was only one chance in a hundred of having obtained this result by chance alone. And a very similar finding was obtained in another study. So manipulation of the wording of the question in such a way as to vary the emphasis placed on the total class did affect difficulty.

To look at the effect of varying emphasis on the contrast between sub-classes McGarrigle used different material. This time he had a small teddy bear, a toy table and a toy chair, laid out in a line. Four discs, referred to as 'steps', separated the teddy bear from the chair; a further two discs lay between the chair and the table thus:

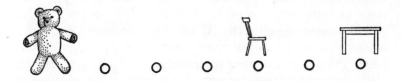

This material gave McGarrigle a number of advantages. The main one was that he could vary the perceptual contrast between the sub-classes (all the steps could be the same colour, or alternatively the steps from Teddy to the chair could be one colour while the steps from the chair to the table could be another) and at the same time he could vary the way of referring to the steps, either mentioning colour or leaving it out. So he could compare the effects of perceptual variables with those of linguistic ones.

In the first experiment which McGarrigle carried out with this material, the four steps to the chair were red, the two others were white. The child was told that Teddy always walked on these steps to go to his chair or to his table. Two forms of question were then used:

1 Are there more red steps to go to the chair or more steps to go to the table?

2 Are there more steps to go to the chair or more steps to go to the table?

Of a group of 32 children, 38 per cent (12 children)

answered question 1 correctly while 66 per cent (21 children) answered question 2 correctly. This difference was statistically significant, there being about two chances in a hundred that it might arise by chance alone.

In this experiment *perceptual* contrast was always present; but one form of question referred to this contrast, while the other did not.

Let us look now at what happens when there is no perceptual contrast. If all the steps are white, it is still possible to include the colour adjective in one case and exclude it in the other. McGarrigle did this in a second study, using a different group of children, but now the variation in question form was found to make a much smaller difference. When the adjective 'white' was included ('Are there more white steps to go to the chair or more steps to go to the table?') 56 per cent of the children answered correctly. When it was omitted ('Are there more steps to go to the chair or more steps to go to the table?') 69 per cent of them answered correctly. This difference was not statistically significant, that is, we are not justified in concluding that one of the questions was genuinely more difficult for the children than the other.

Even though there was no difference between the question forms it might have proved to be the case that the absence of *perceptual* contrast would make this task easier overall than the earlier task where some of the steps were red. Notice that no such effect was found. The basic question: *Are there more steps to go to the chair or more steps to go to the table?* was answered correctly by almost the same proportion of children (drawn from a different group of subjects) whether the steps were all the same colour or whether they were sharply contrasted.

This is an important set of findings. Neither perceptual contrast nor change of wording alone made a difference. The two together made a considerable one. Also it is interesting to notice that the change of wording which made such a difference when perceptual contrast was present was a very slight one: the insertion or omission of a single adjective.

The 'steps' task may seem to be rather different from the standard Piagetian class-inclusion one, but it is closely analogous to a variant used by Piaget himself. Sometimes he took as material a set of beads – all of them wooden, most of them brown, a few of them white – and in this case he would sometimes ask which would make a longer necklace: the brown beads or the wooden beads. And the young child would typically answer: 'The brown beads because there are only two white ones.' But this material, unlike McGarrigle's, did not make it possible to manipulate the relevant linguistic and perceptual variables so as to lessen contrast between the sub-classes. Perceptual contrast was necessarily present: the beads could not be all of one colour or there would be no way of referring to the sub-classes. And by the same token the perceptual contrast always had to be marked in the language of the question. Thus the situation was the one which McGarrigle has shown to be maximally difficult for the child.

McGarrigle, on the other hand, was able to find a form of wording even easier than any of those we have discussed so far. He asked the question: 'Is it further for Teddy to go to the chair, or further to go to the table?' Now at this point one may not properly speak of *class* inclusion, but rather of the in-clusion of one distance within another. However, what is particularly interesting is that not only was this question form easier (72 per cent success in one study, 84 per cent in another), but when the other questions were repeated after this one they were considerably facilitated. The question 'Are there more steps to go to the chair or more steps to go to the table?' was now answered correctly by 88 per cent of the children and even the 'red steps' version led to 53 per cent success.

It seems as if the question that asks *which is further?* helps the children to grasp what it is that the experimenter intends them to consider; and once they have grasped this they may be able to hang on to it even in the face of wordings which would otherwise tend to lead them astray.

However, a fair number of children continue to find the 'red steps' wording intractable: in the experiment we have been considering 47 per cent persisted in answering in terms of sub-class comparison when 'red steps' were mentioned. This makes one begin to wonder whether their mode of interpretation has anything to do with their grasp of the inclusion situation *per se* or whether it stems from something much more general.

To decide this, it is necessary to look at similar question forms in contexts where inclusion does not arise. McGarrigle did so, both with the toy cows and horses and with Teddy and his steps.

He arranged black and white toy cows and horses on either side of a wall facing one another thus:

```
                    Cows
      B        B        W        W
   ─────────────────────────────────
      B        B        B        W
                   Horses
```

The children were then asked a number of questions of which the following is an example:

Are there more cows or more black horses?

Of 36 children only 5 (14 per cent) answered this correctly. Why were the others wrong?

It is evident that Piaget's explanation will not serve. There is no question here of inclusion or of having to hold on simultaneously to a whole and to the parts that compose the whole. What the children are doing is, however, clear. For the most part they are comparing the black horses with the black cows, for they make remarks like: 'There's more black horses 'cos there's only two black cows.'

A version of the 'steps' experiment which did not involve inclusion led to a similar finding. This time Teddy, the chair and the table did not lie along a straight line, but were arranged as in the diagram on page 49. So the 'steps to the chair' did not constitute a subset of the 'steps to the table'. The questions were exactly as in the original 'inclusion' version, namely:

1 Are there more red steps to go to the chair or more steps to go to the table?

2 Are there more steps to go to the chair or more steps to go to the table?

And, just as before, question 1 was significantly harder. The children's remarks showed that sometimes they compared 'red steps to the chair' with the sub-set of red steps to the table. Sometimes, however, the comparison made was with the sub-set of white steps. And occasionally it seemed that the children were answering a rather different question, for they would say things like: 'There's red all along there [to the chair] but there's white there,' or 'They're all red there.' It was as if they were answering a question which ran something like this: 'Are more of the steps to the table red – or are more of the steps to the chair red?' – a question, that is, which asked for some sort of comparison of proportions.

In any event, the questions the children were answering were frequently not the questions the experimenter had asked. The children's interpretations did not correspond to the experimenter's intention; nor could they be regarded as normal, given the rules of the language. The children did not know what the experimenter meant; and one is tempted to say they did not strictly appear to know what the language meant. Or, if that seems too strong, one must at least say that something other than 'the rules of the language' was shaping their interpretation – something perhaps like an expectation about the question that would be asked, an expectation that could be influenced by the nature of the experimental material.

49

However, it is essential to notice that we may not conclude that the children were, in some general way, not *bothering* to attend to the language – for we must recall the dramatic effect, in some of the studies, of the inclusion or omission of a single adjective.

5. What *Is* and What *Must Be*

Piaget has not been alone in claiming that young children are incapable of inferences which, to an adult, seem elementary. From a type of psychological theory utterly opposed to his own, precisely the same conclusion has been drawn. One of the most eminent of the associationist – or behaviourist – psychologists, Clark Hull, claimed that the essence of reasoning lies in the putting together of two 'behaviour segments' in some novel way, never actually performed before, so as to reach a goal. Serious objections can be raised to this way of defining reasoning but let us accept it for the moment and look at what happens if we study children's thinking in a way guided by the Hullian conception.

When Hull spoke of the joining of two 'behaviour segments' he spoke against a background of studies of rats learning to run mazes – studies of a kind so popular with the behaviourists. A 'behaviour segment' was then exemplified by the running from one point in the maze to another.

The claim was as follows. Suppose you arrange the maze as in the diagram on page 52. Now suppose that a rat learns to run from A to B to get a small reward; and from A to C to get an equally small reward; and from C to D to get a much bigger reward (all of these bits of learning taking place on separate occasions). If you then place him at Point A and he chooses the path A→C→D, instead of the path A→B, he must be *reasoning* that you can get to D that way, for he has never actually *been* from A to D that way before.

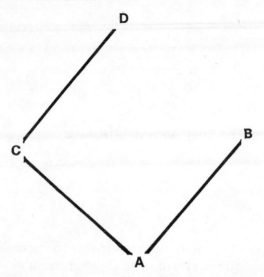

Of course, there is a 50/50 chance of taking that road randomly, with no reasoning at all. But if a large number of rats were all to take it, that would be evidence of rodent reasoning.

In fact this evidence has not been obtained. Rats don't, apparently, figure things out in this way.

More strangely, evidence has been obtained which makes it look as if children under the age of seven don't either.

Two followers of Clark Hull, Howard and Tracy Kendler, devised a test for children that was explicitly based on Hullian principles. However, it did not involve running a maze. Instead the children were given the task of learning to operate a machine so as to get a toy. In order to succeed they had to go through a two-stage sequence corresponding to the segments of the maze. The children were trained on each stage separately. The stages consisted merely of pressing the correct one of two buttons to get a marble; and of inserting a marble into a small hole to release the toy.

The Kendlers found that the children could learn the separate bits readily enough. Given the task of getting a marble by pressing the button they could get the marble; given the task of getting a toy when a marble was handed to them, they could use the marble. (All they had to do was put it in a hole.) But they did not for the most part 'integrate', to use the Kendlers' terminology. They did not press the button to get the marble and then proceed without further help to use the marble to get the toy. So the Kendlers concluded that they were incapable, like the rats, of deductive reasoning. This work was done in the 1960s. No wonder Chomsky could so readily convince people of the need to postulate a highly specific device for the acquisition of language.

On the other hand, the Kendlers' results are bound to seem deeply puzzling to anyone who has watched children playing in a nursery or listened to their conversation, and who really brings the two kinds of data together in his mind.

Here is a striking example of the kind of reasoning of which children seem to be capable if one observes their spontaneous behaviour, by contrast with their behaviour when they are being tested.

This exchange happened to be tape-recorded, so it can be quoted very accurately. It took place shortly after the death of Donald Campbell when he was trying to break the world water speed record, and some months after a visit by a research worker called Robin Campbell to the school where the conversation took place. The speakers were a little girl of five and another research worker.

CHILD: 'Is that Mr Campbell who came here – *dead*?' (Dramatic stress on the word 'dead'.)
RESEARCH WORKER: 'No, I'm quite sure he isn't dead.' (Much surprised.)
CHILD: 'Well, there must be two Mr Campbells then, because Mr Campbell's dead, under the water.'

This child has put together, if not two 'behaviour segments', two quite distinct pieces of information: *Mr Campbell who came here is not dead* and *Mr Campbell is dead*, and has drawn a valid conclusion, which she states as a necessary consequence: '. . . there *must be* two Mr Campbells then . . .' Her reasoning involves the understanding that the existence of a living person is incompatible with the death of that same person. So if Mr Campbell is dead and Mr Campbell is alive, there simply must be two of them!

How can it be that children of five are capable of reasoning like this, yet can fail to 'integrate' two very simple bits of separately learned behaviour in a task such as the Kendlers used?

The mystery at first appears to deepen when we learn, from Michael Cole and his colleagues, that adults in an African culture apparently cannot do the Kendlers' task either. But it lessens, on the other hand, when we learn that a task was devised which was strictly analogous to the Kendlers' one but much easier for the African adults to handle.

Instead of the button-pressing machine, Cole used a locked box and two differently coloured match-boxes, one of which contained a key that would open the box. Notice that there are still two behaviour segments ('open the right match-box to get the key' and 'use the key to open the box') so the task seems formally to be the same. But psychologically it is quite different. Now the subject is dealing not with a strange machine but with familiar meaningful objects; and it is clear to him what he is meant to do. It then turns out that the difficulty of 'integration' is greatly reduced.

Recent work by Simon Hewson is of great interest here for it shows that, for young children too, the difficulty lies not in the inferential processes which the task demands, but in certain perplexing features of the apparatus and the procedure. When these are changed in ways which do not at all affect the inferential nature of the problem, then five-year-old children solve the problem as well as college students did in the Kendlers' own experiments.

Hewson made two crucial changes. First, he replaced the button-pressing mechanism in the side panels by drawers in these panels which the child could open and shut. This took away the mystery from the first stage of training. Then he helped the child to understand that there was no 'magic' about the specific marble which, during the second stage of training, the experimenter handed to him so that he could pop it in the hole and get the reward. A child understands nothing, after all, about how a marble put into a hole can open a little door. How is he to know that any other marble of similar size will do just as well? Yet he must assume this if he is to solve the problem. Hewson made the functional equivalence of different marbles clear by playing a 'swapping game' with the children.

These two modifications together produced a jump in success rates from 30 per cent to 90 per cent for five-year-olds and from 35 per cent to 72·5 per cent for four-year-olds. For three-year-olds, for reasons that are still in need of clarification, no improvement – rather a slight drop in performance – resulted from the change.

We may conclude, then, that children experience very real difficulty when faced with the Kendler apparatus; but this difficulty cannot be taken as proof that they are incapable of deductive reasoning.

With this conclusion in mind, let us see now how children behave in a very different type of situation.

It is highly informative to listen to the comments children make and the questions they ask when they listen to stories. In this situation a rich harvest of evidence of reasoning may be reaped.

Here are a few examples:

'What a lot of things he's taking! He wouldn't have . . . he's only got two hands and he wouldn't have space for his two hands to carry all these things.'

(*Premises*: (1) Peter has more to carry than two hands can carry; (2) Peter has only two hands. *Conclusion*: It is not possible for Peter to carry all that he is represented as carrying. Implied criticism of the story.)

'She must have eaten all her food on the other day.'

(*Premises*: (1) Houses normally have food in them; (2) This house has no food. *Conclusion*: The food must have been all eaten up.)

'But how can it be [that they are getting married]? You have to have a man too.' (The book contains an illustration of a wedding in which the man looks rather like a woman. The child thinks it is a picture of two women.)

(*Premises*: (1) You need a man for a wedding; (2) There is no man in the picture. *Conclusion*: It can't be a wedding.)

'I think you have missed a page. You didn't say that he cut out the leather.'

(*Premises*: (1) There is a page on which the story tells of cutting out leather; (2) No reference has been made to cutting out leather. *Conclusion*: A page has been missed.)

CHILD: 'You're not looking.'
TEACHER: 'Pardon?'
CHILD: 'Why are you not reading it?'
TEACHER: 'Because I know it.'

(*Premises*: (1) When you read a book you look at it; (2) The teacher is not looking at the book. *Conclusion*: She is not reading the book.)

It is impossible to take account of this evidence and at the same time to maintain that children under the age of six or seven are incapable of reasoning deductively. So if sometimes – as in certain experimental situations – they do not appear to reason deductively, we must look more closely at what is happening. If we cannot get children to reason when we contrive experiments, whereas we can observe them reasoning spontaneously, then we must ask why.

It turns out, however, that in spite of the findings of Piaget and the Kendlers and some others, it is not impossible to get children to reason in the contrived circumstances of an experiment. It is harder but it is not impossible.

Barbara Wallington conducted a series of experiments where the task was to find a toy in one – or more than one – of a set of boxes which might or might not have stars on the lids. She designed her studies with great care and a desire to give children every chance to grasp what it was that she wanted of them. The results were revealing.

The children were given information which they could use to guide their search. For instance, they might be told: 'If there is a star on the box, then there is a wee animal in the box,' or: 'If there is no star, then there is a wee animal in the box.' After hearing a statement of this kind, they were asked to predict which boxes would contain a toy and to check whether they were right.

The pattern of the children's choices and the nature of their answers when they were asked why they had made the choices showed very clearly that many of them were engaging in processes of strict reasoning in the sense that they were using the experimenter's statement as a basis from which to deduce conclusions. They very rarely drew all the conclusions which would be judged correct by the canons of traditional formal logic – but neither did a group of adults to whom the same task was given. The older children (and 'older' in this case means between four years three months and four years eleven months) frequently responded in just the same way as the adults, taking 'if there is a star . . .' to mean 'if *and only if* there is a star . . .' and reasoning accordingly. Some of the children were also able to give explanations very like those of the adults, using such expressions as: *it must be, it has to be.* Here are two examples, by way of illustration: 'When there's no star, there's supposed to be a wee animal in the box.' 'It must be in there [box with no star] if it's not in there [starred box].' In this last case the given statement had been: 'If there is a star, then there is no wee animal.'

Notice that these justifications were made after the children had indicated which boxes they were choosing but before they had been allowed to open them.

From children under four years, such responses as these were relatively uncommon. But even the youngest children did not behave randomly. They tended to have systematic search strategies, even if these were as primitive and unrelated to the experimenter's words as starting with a box at one end and working along the row.

Further evidence that, even in experimental situations, children can sometimes give proof of their ability to reason is now being obtained. Peter Bryant and Paul Harris have each independently looked at the child's ability to engage in the kind of inference which is concerned with transitive relations such as 'equal to' or 'greater than'. (This is yet another form of inference which Piaget regards as criterial for operational thought and which, therefore, according to his theory, is not normally to be found in children under age seven.) To illustrate the findings of Bryant and of Harris we shall look at two studies – one by each of them – on the child's ability to compare the size of two objects by means of some intermediary – which means in effect that the intermediary is serving as a measuring instrument.

Harris and his colleagues showed four-year-old children two strips of paper placed about three feet apart. The strips differed in length by about a quarter of an inch – too small a difference to be perceptible. Thus when the children were asked which strip was longer approximately half their judgements were correct, this being, of course, the result that would be expected by chance alone. Then a third strip of paper, equal in length to one of the other two, was produced; and it was briefly placed alongside each of the others in turn. The question was then repeated. And now most of the children gave the correct answer. This seems to show clearly that they were capable of understanding measurement, which is to say that they were able to make inferences of the form: if A equals B and if B is longer than C, then A must be longer than C.

Bryant and Kopytynska have reached conclusions similar to those of Harris about the ability of young children to make measurements. They used simple but ingenious equipment to show that, though young children often do not spontaneously measure things which they can compare visually, they do frequently use a measuring instrument when visual comparison is impossible. They gave their subjects two black wooden blocks, each with a hole in it, and asked them to find out whether one of the holes was deeper than the other. It was quite impossible to see the bottom of the holes. Between the two blocks, the experimenters had placed a wooden stick which the child could use as a measuring instrument if he chose to do so. Even in conditions where no mention of the stick was made, many children used the stick as a means of solving the problem.

Let us take stock. From the evidence we have been considering the main points to emerge are these:

1. Children are not at any stage as egocentric as Piaget has claimed. For all human beings, the taking of another point of view requires a certain effort, and the difficulty is bound to vary from one situation to another in many complex ways. But the gap between children and adults is not so great in this respect as has recently been widely believed.

2. Children are not so limited in ability to reason deductively as Piaget—and others—have claimed. This ability shows itself most markedly in some aspects of their spontaneous

behaviour—and we have seen that it reveals itself with great clarity in the comments they make while listening to stories. But it can be demonstrated also in the contrived situation of an experiment from about the age of four, if not sooner, even though many experiments have failed to elicit it. At least from age four, then, we must again acknowledge that the supposed gap between children and adults is less than many people have claimed.

3. A child's ability to learn language is indeed something at which we may wonder. But his language-learning skills are not isolated from the rest of his mental growth. There is no reason to suppose that he is born with an 'acquisition device' which enables him to structure and make sense of the language he hears while failing to structure and make sense of the other features of his environment. On the contrary it now looks as though he first makes sense of situations (and perhaps especially those involving human intention) and then uses *this* kind of understanding to help him to make sense of what is said to him.

It appears, then, that the theories about the growth of language and thinking which have been most influential over recent years are, in important respects, ill-founded. This does *not* mean that these theories are wrong in their entirety.

Nor should we conclude that, because children turn out to be in some respects closer to adults than has been supposed, they are really just like them after all. It may simply be that we have to look for the differences elsewhere.

6. What is Said and What is Meant

'What is said is slippery stuff.' (P. Ziff).

'Was anybody with you in the boat?'
'No, there weren't.'
'Then what was that grandson of yours doing?'
'Oh, him? He was with me. I thought you meant
was there somebody else, that didn't ought to have
been there.' (Dorothy L. Sayers).

The intellectually sophisticated adult within our kind of cultural tradition – the sort of person who teaches in schools, or studies children's thinking and language – is conscious of language as a formal system in terms of which one can represent the world. Such a person has come to think of language as having what has been called 'timeless meaning' – that is to say, meaning which can be considered apart from any particular context of use, meaning which is not totally embedded in events, in the ongoing flow of 'real life'. It is possible, once the sophisticated view of language has developed, to construct an isolated sentence and ask: 'What does it mean?' But so far as we can tell it is alien to the primitive or 'natural' way of dealing with language to treat it in isolation in this manner. Recall the example of the Indian who said that he could not translate 'The white man shot six bears today' because no white man could do so.*

---

* Of course, even intellectually sophisticated adults do not ordinarily *use* language without relying heavily on context (see page 69). And on the other hand, we must beware of assuming that all the peoples whom we are apt to call 'primitive' can simply be lumped together. For instance, Mary Douglas, speaking of the Dogon people, tells us that 'the intellectual unity which they confer on experience is derived from reflecting on the nature, power and effects of language.' However, she goes on immediately to raise the question whether 'this would presuppose a degree of self-consciousness about the processes of thought which would lift their culture clear out of the class of primitives.'

In previous chapters we have been considering some short-comings of recent theories about the growth of the mind. All of these shortcomings can be seen as related to a failure to pay enough attention to the difference between language as it is spontaneously used and interpreted by a child and language as it has come to be conceived of by those who develop the theories.

Chomsky obviously thinks of the child's task as that of learning the sort of thing which language is for Chomsky himself. And so indeed it is – in the long run. But in the shorter run, during the early years of life, it may be something very different.

For Piagetian theory, the effect of the adult conception is less direct, for Piaget is less concerned with language learning. And when he does talk about it he is much more sensitive to differences between what language has become for the adult and what language is for the child in the early stages. However when he himself, as an experimenter, *uses* language, as part of his method for studying children's thinking, he appears to lose sight of the significance of this issue.

Perhaps the best known of all Piagetian tasks are those called 'conservation tests'. There are many such tests – tests of conservation of number, weight, length, volume and so on, but conservation of length will serve as an example, for the principles are common to them all.

The test has three stages. First the child is shown two sticks of equal length placed thus: ═══════ in exact alignment. He is then asked whether they are the same length. It is essential that he should agree to equality of length at this stage, otherwise the test cannot legitimately proceed.

Next, one of the two sticks is moved (normally by the adult experimenter) so that the alignment is destroyed, thus: ────────. The experimenter usually explicitly invites the child to pay attention to this transformation by saying, 'Now watch what I do.'

The third stage then consists simply in repeating the original question – 'Are they the same length?' or whatever was the precise wording – after the transformation of the second stage is complete.

The essential principles common to all variants of

conservation tests are the following:

(a) The initial equality of the critical attribute (length, weight, etc.) is combined with perceptual similarity (sticks placed so that their ends are aligned, balls of plasticine which are the same shape as well as the same weight, etc.).

(b) The child is questioned about the initial equality of the critical attribute, and accepts it.

(c) A transformation occurs which destroys the perceptual similarity without affecting the critical attribute.

(d) The child is again questioned about the critical attribute.

If, on the second questioning, the child still affirms the equality of the critical attribute then he is said to 'conserve' length or weight or whatever the attribute may be. Otherwise he is said to fail to conserve or to be a 'non-conserver'.

Children under the age of seven commonly fail to conserve when given the standard tests. Piaget takes this, once more, as evidence of failure to decentre and of failure to reason. The correct answer, he says, depends on the ability to make an inference from two premises – namely: (1) these things were the same length (or weight etc.) before; (2) nothing has been done which alters length (or weight etc.) – to the conclusion: therefore they must be the same length now, even though they look different. Failure to reason in this way is held to stem from an inability to decentre, both with regard to the immediate perceptual situation and with regard to the relation between one moment in time and a succeeding one. The child centres on one feature of the immediate situation and neglects others – for instance he calls one stick longer because it projects further at one side, failing to take account of the compensating fact that it projects less far at the other. Also he centres on the present moment, failing to think back to how things were before, failing to see that one act is in principle *reversible*, and that the sticks could be pushed back into alignment again. The ability to make use of this principle of reversibility in one's thinking is, for Piaget, one of the main signs of having reached the stage of concrete operational thinking. (See Appendix.)

Leaving explanation aside, what actually happens when a

'non-conserving' response occurs? It amounts to this: in a short space of time, the child gives two conflicting answers to what, for an adult, is the same question with 'the same meaning'. But suppose that the child is not concerned to weigh specially what the words of the question mean in isolation. Suppose he is rather interpreting the whole situation: what the experimenter says, what he does, what he may reasonably be thought to intend. Now recall that at stage two the experimenter draws attention to an action whereby he changes the array that the child is considering. 'Watch this,' he says. Is it not then reasonable that the child should think this change will be relevant to what follows – to the next question which will be asked?*

Susan Rose and Marion Blank considered this possibility and asked what would happen if the child were given a 'one-judgement version' of the conservation task – that is, a version where the first question was omitted and the child was questioned only *after* seeing the rearrangement of the objects. For they reasoned that the child may take the repetition of the question as 'a cue that he should alter his first judgement so as to acknowledge the change he has just witnessed.' They found that six-year-old children made fewer errors not only on the one-judgement task itself but also on a standard conservation test which they were given a week later. So they concluded that contextual cues which an adult would regard as insignificant may not seem so to a child.

One way to describe the difference between child and adult would then be to say that it lies in the amount of weight that is given to *sheer linguistic form*. The question seems to be whether the meaning of the language carries enough weight

* Rochel Gelman noted a further fact: that when something changes, even in a totally impersonal situation, the changing feature tends to attract our attention. She devised a training programme aimed at getting children to realize that in the conservation tasks the change was nonetheless irrelevant and to be ignored. At the end of this programme there was very marked improvement in performance on the tasks in which the children were specifically trained (length and number conservation). There was also evidence of some improvement on other conservation tasks on which no training had been given.

to over-ride the meaning of the situation. Does the language have priority? Can it over-ride the reasonable expectation?

Another way of trying to determine whether the young child's response to conservation questions results from his having a tendency to give priority to the meaning of the *situation* was devised by James McGarrigle. McGarrigle's idea was to alter the events of stage two in such a way as to make them seem accidental – not brought about deliberately by the experimenter, thus not relevant to what he meant when he moved on to stage three and repeated the initial question. To achieve this, McGarrigle introduced a character called 'Naughty Teddy' – a small teddy bear who was liable to emerge from his box, swoop over the experimental material, disarrange it and thus 'mess up the game'.

McGarrigle found that this version of the task – where the transformation was ostensibly accidental – was dealt with much more successfully than the traditional version: many more children between the ages of four and six 'conserved' – that is, continued to say that the crucial attribute was the same.*

This finding is dramatic and it seems to be very difficult to explain in Piagetian terms. On his view of the matter it is impossible to see why the *agent* of the transformation should be critical.

However, we have to take note of the fact that, even when 'Naughty Teddy' was the agent, some children (roughly 30 per cent of a group of 80 children) failed to conserve. What determined their responding?

It is a feature of Piaget's explanation that the 'look of the thing' is important. Consider what it would be like, at stage

* This finding has been replicated in an unpublished study carried out by Julie Dockrell at the University of Stirling. She did not find such a marked effect, especially among the younger subjects, but she does report an overall difference between the 'Naughty Teddy' task and the traditional task that was great enough to have only one chance in a thousand of occurring by chance alone. Also her study confirms a finding in the original study that children who are given the 'Naughty Teddy' task first and then the traditional task perform significantly better than children who do the two tasks in the reverse order.

three in a conservation task, for a child who could not decentre. He would notice the projecting end of one stick, or some other aspect of the perceptual differences that had been introduced at stage two. He would not be able to balance or cancel this by reference either to the compensatory perceptual idfference (which would of course always be present) or to the original perceptual similarity of stage one. So, being dominated by the perception of difference, he would respond 'No' when asked: 'Are they the same?'

It is possible, without invoking inability to decentre, to allow that something like 'domination by the look of the thing' may occur. For the same sort of 'domination' may undoubtedly be produced in other ways. We have already seen that conflict may arise between expectations about what question is going to be asked and the linguistic form of the question when it actually comes along. So far we have been talking about expectations derived from some assessment of the experimenter's intentions. But it is of course entirely possible for there to be expectations which do not depend on these.

To illustrate this, we now turn to the findings of other studies. The first of these was conducted by Peter Lloyd and myself, the second by James McGarrigle and myself.

In the first, the task for the children was to judge whether certain statements were true or false – but these terms were not used. Nor did the statements ostensibly come from an adult, in case the adult's authority would be too great and would affect the judgements. Instead we had a large toy panda which could be made to appear to speak. The children were then asked to help the panda by telling him if he was right or if he was wrong. This they did with evident enjoyment.

The children – and ostensibly the panda – were then shown an array of four garages, joined together in a row, and a set of toy cars. Sometimes there were three cars in the set, sometimes five. And among the statements to be judged were these:

All the cars are in the garages and
All the garages have cars in them.

When 'all the cars' amounted to three, these three were indeed all put inside the garages, so the first statement was true.

But of course in this situation the second statement was false: one garage was empty.

On the other hand, when the total set of cars was five in number these could not all be in the garages. In this case four were put in and the fifth was left sitting in full view outside. So now the truth values of the two sentences were reversed: the first was false and the second was true.

But this was not the opinion of all the children. We found a pattern of response which at the time we had in no way anticipated. Some of the children would hold *both* sentences to be false when there were only three cars and both of them to be true when there were five. So when there were three cars in four garages they would tell the panda he was wrong to say the cars were all in them; and when there was one car sitting outside four occupied garages they would tell him he was right to say that they were all in them.

One might suppose at first sight that the children did not know the meaning of *all*; but we had other evidence to suggest that this explanation would not do. For instance, if it was a question of judging whether all the garage doors were shut, they could do it perfectly well.

Another possible explanation, at least for the three car situation, was that the children did not take *all the cars* to mean all the cars they had been shown (though they had been shown them with careful emphasis on the fact that these were 'all the cars'), but rather they took the phrase to mean all the cars which properly belonged with the set of garages – something like *all the cars which ought to be there*. And notice that if we say: 'Have you put all the knives and forks on the table?' we are at least as likely to mean 'all the knives and forks that are going to be needed' as 'all the knives and forks that are kept in the drawer'. Which meaning we choose will depend on the total context – on such considerations as whether we are clearing out the drawer or preparing to have a meal.

At any rate, it was evident in the experiment we are discussing that the children responded as if what they were looking at and attending to all the time was the fullness of the garages. The statement which they actually judged, irrespective of the variations in linguistic form, was: 'All the garages are

66

full.' And when they had told the panda that he was wrong and were going on to explain why, it was nearly always fullness that they spoke about. If there were three cars in four garages and the panda said 'All the cars are in the garages', the child would say something like: 'You're wrong, 'cos there's an empty one.' Watching the children and listening to them, one had the powerful impression that the empty garage was somehow *salient* for them, and that they interpreted everything they heard in ways affected by this salience.

So we have to take into account that what the child expects to hear is liable to be influenced not only by things which give him clues about the speaker's intentions but also by more impersonal features of the situation he is considering. The second study pointed to this same kind of conclusion. It was a study of a closely related kind, but now the child answered questions instead of judging statements right or wrong.

Once again toy cars and garages were used. This time the cars were arranged on two shelves, one directly above the other. This was because a comparison was now to be called for and we wanted the children to see both arrays clearly. On one shelf there were five cars, on the other four. These were placed in one-to-one correspondence, starting from the left, so that in one row an extra car always projected to the right. The children were asked: 'Are there more cars on this shelf or more cars on this shelf?' And to this question they usually responded readily and correctly. But we then introduced a change. Over each row of cars we placed a row of garages. (These had no floors and they could be added or removed with ease.) The row of four cars was enclosed by a row of four garages, so that all the garages in this row were occupied. The row of five cars was enclosed by a row of six garages, so that one garage was empty. (For half of the children the two conditions were presented in reverse order: first the garages were present, then they were taken away.) The question was then repeated – and about a third of the children changed their judgements, saying that now the shelf with four cars had more cars on it than the shelf with five!

What are we to make of this kind of response? Notice, first, an interesting parallel to what happens in a classical conservation test. (See page 61.) The child gives one answer to a question; something irrelevant (to 'the meaning' of the words in the question) is changed; and now the child gives a different answer.

Does the child have a whole set of different meanings for the words, then, among which he alternates? If so, he certainly does not alternate randomly, or else we could hardly get whole groups of children shifting meanings in the same way. It must be that something apart from the words themselves is constraining the child's interpretation.

In the second study, as in the ordinary conservation task, some consideration of speaker's intention may have affected the outcome. But when the garages are placed over the cars, why should the children think they are meant to attend to *fullness* rather than, say, length of the row of garages?

Also, in the first study involving the toy panda, it is not so easy to invoke intention as an explanation. Here it seems that the child's own *reading* of the situation is what we must look to. It seems that what he attends to is fullness, even though the words he hears do not direct him to it.

Underlying this suggestion there is a whole set of very fundamental notions about the ways in which we relate to the world. Of these, the most important is the idea that this relation is *active* on our part from the beginning. We do not just sit and wait for the world to impinge on us. We try actively to interpret it, to make sense of it. We grapple with it, we construe it intellectually, *we represent it to ourselves*.

Another way to put this is to say that we are, by nature, questioners. We approach the world wondering about it, entertaining hypotheses which we are eager to check. And we direct our questions not just to other people but to ourselves, giving ourselves the job of finding the answer by direct exploration of the world. In this way we build up what it is fashionable to call a *model* of the world – a kind of system of inner representations, the value of which is to help us to anticipate events and be ready to deal with them.

The expectations thus generated are known to be powerful things. The present suggestion is that when a child hears words that refer to a situation which he is at the same time perceiving, his interpretation of the words is influenced by the expectations which he brings to the situation. If he is disposed to construe the situation in a certain way, giving salience to some features of it rather than others, then this predisposition will influence what he takes the words to mean.

At the same time, we must not forget that the influence can work both ways. Thus it is also true that the way a situation is described will have an effect on how the child construes it. Robert Grieve and his colleagues have recently carried out an important study in which pre-school children were given two plain cardboard boxes, one larger than the other. These boxes were sometimes referred to as 'the big box' and 'the little box'; sometimes as 'the table' and 'the cup'; sometimes as 'the bath' and 'the baby' and so on. The children were given instructions asking them to put one object *in*, *on* or *under* the other; and the most significant finding was that responses to the instructions were affected by the ways in which the boxes were named. This was so even at the very early age of two-and-a-half years.

So we reach this conclusion: when a child interprets what we say to him his interpretation is influenced by at least three things (and the ways in which these interact with each other) – his knowledge of the language, his assessment of what we intend (as indicated by our non-linguistic behaviour), and the manner in which he would represent the physical situation to himself if we were not there at all.

The question then arises whether in this respect the processes of interpretation in which children engage differ from those of adults.

It may be that much of the time they do not differ greatly. Certainly assessment of intention and of physical situation also affects the way in which adults communicate.

We do not, in our ordinary conversations with one another, attend to 'pure linguistic meaning'. Ziff, in a book called *Understanding Understanding*, gives a number of examples of this. For instance, if we heard the following statement made about a game of football: 'No one got in without a ticket', we would not interpret this with strict attention to 'the meaning' of 'no one'. In other words, we would not be led to conclude that all the employees and players had tickets or else were refused entry. When we interpret utterances we make continual – and usually unconscious – use of knowledge about states of affairs in addition to knowledge about language.

However, it remains true that we experience surprise when we learn of the sorts of response by children which have just been discussed. And from older subjects these responses are indeed not obtained. So what is it that changes?

There are several possible sources of difference:

(a) The young child's knowledge of the language is less, or he is less confident about it. So he gives more weight to cues of non-linguistic kinds where he is on surer ground. (It might be that this difference arises only in situations where the child's language is inadequate – or it might be that children habitually give more weight than adults to cues of this kind.)

(b) The child has not learned to distinguish between situations where he is supposed to give primacy to the language, and situations where he is not.

When an adult *tests* a child the situation tends to be of the former kind. But perhaps the child does not know this; and certainly it has not been common practice for the adult to tell him. However, in the 'talking panda' study the children's task was to judge what the doll *said* – and considerable care was taken to make this explicit. Yet the results were not substantially different from those in related studies. So this brings us to the third possibility.

(c) The child is not able to pay scrupulous attention to the language in its own right – or at least he finds it very difficult.

We shall return later to the question of what might make this harder or easier to do.

First, however, it is necessary to consider evidence from two different sources which may seem to be at variance with the argument we have been developing.

This argument has led us to the conclusion that, when situations arise where the interpretation of words is not in accord with some other expectation, then the words tend not to win the day. There is, however, one study where 'word meaning' does seem to win the day – with grotesque results.

Robin Campbell took 24 children between the ages of three and five and told them a story from which the following are extracts:

She would like to work in the big post office but she works in a *branch* ... As they were driving along they saw a *hare* run across a field ... Then they got back into the car and drove to the seaside. When they got there they went for a walk along the *quay* ... 'Look at this castle', said Jane's Daddy. 'The oldest *wing* is over 500 years old.' ... They got held up behind a lot of other cars, all going very slowly. 'I hope we get out of this *jam* soon', said Jane's Daddy.

The children were asked to draw the hare, the quay, the wing, etc. Many of them drew a hair (or a head of hair), a key, a bird's wing, etc. They were also questioned – for instance, as follows:

'What does a hare look like?'   *Child touches hair.*
'Do you think it would be running across a field?' '*Yes.*'
'What sort of thing is a quay? What's a quay for?'   '*For opening doors.*'
'Do you think they could walk along a quay?'   *Child nods.*

Overall, no less than 31 per cent of the responses were of this curious kind.

We have repeatedly seen that young children's interpretations of language may be powerfully influenced by context, so that they fail to show adequate respect for the words themselves. But now here we have evidence that a situation can be found where the opposite occurs. The interpretations depend on words considered in isolation and without adequate respect for context. Thus the words *hare*, *quay*, *wing*, etc. are given their usual interpretation in contexts where this makes no sense. Why?

We should notice at least four things. First, the context was that of story-telling; and in the stories commonly told to children many strange and wonderful events occur. Second, the children were probably highly familiar with the critical words – or rather with the same-sounding words: 'hair', 'key', etc. – in a sense which was very hard to reconcile with the story context, and they were probably quite unfamiliar with them in any other sense. Third, no immediate context of a visible, non-verbal kind was there to influence the outcome

– no cars or garages, no pairs of sticks, no toy cows or horses. Finally – and by the same token – the experimenter's questions were not about any such context. Rather the critical words were picked out from the (verbal) context and questions were asked about *them*: 'What sort of thing is a quay?' etc. In all these respects, the situation was very different from those considered earlier in this chapter.

It remains true – and highly noteworthy – that instead of drawing some kind of animal running across a field, some sort of seaside path that people might walk along and some reasonable part of a castle, a considerable number of the children drew hair, a key, a bird's wing, and then produced – or at least agreed with – nonsensical propositions. And the same tendency to acquiesce in the bizarre is reported in a recent study by Martin Hughes and Robert Grieve. When they asked children (aged between five and seven this time) unanswerable questions like 'Is milk bigger than water?' they did not get rejection of the question (except from the youngest child in the group – a boy of barely five – who 'grinned his head off'!). Rather they got solemn answers and justifications for these answers, like: 'Milk is bigger because it's got a colour.'

All developmental psychologists, all teachers of young children – and, come to that, all parents – should surely take note, and beware!

The second kind of evidence which may seem to conflict with the main argument of this chapter is very different. It concerns the relation of the *use* or production of language to comprehension.

The argument we have been developing implies that the ease with which pre-school children often seem to understand what is said to them is misleading if we take it as an indication of skill with language *per se*. Certainly they commonly understand us, but surely it is not our words alone that they are understanding – for they may be shown to be relying heavily on cues of other kinds.

Now it is a fact that pre-school children can often *use* language with much skill and fluency. Recall some of the quotations from their responses to stories in Chapter 5. 'What a lot of things he's taking! He wouldn't have . . . he's only got two hands and he wouldn't have space for his two hands to carry all these things' – and so on. These utterances are at least as complex – syntactically and semantically – as sentences like: 'All the cars are in the garages.' Are we then to say that the ability to *use* language is in advance of the ability to understand it?

At first sight, a positive answer to that question might seem to be nonsense. On the face of it, you cannot use language for successful communication unless you understand it. So the comprehension of an utterance should come before the production of it. And indeed there have been experiments which have been widely interpreted as upholding this kind of claim.

It turns out, however, that it is a considerable over-simplification to say that understanding precedes production. 'Understanding' is a very complex notion, and at least two questions have to be distinguished if confusion is to be avoided. First, does the child understand the words he hears in the sense that they are 'in his vocabulary' – that their meaning is not altogether unknown to him? And secondly, given that this is the case, does he on a given occasion understand the words in their context (linguistic or non-linguistic) in the way in which the speaker means him to do?

It is a common but naïve assumption that the understanding of a word is an all-or-none affair: you either understand it or you don't. But this is not so. Knowledge of word-meaning grows, it undergoes development and change. Also, the process of understanding an utterance does not just depend on the serial addition of one word-meaning to another. It is an active process of structuring and making sense of the whole. Thus the 'correct' interpretation of a word on one occasion is no guarantee of full understanding on another. For instance, Alison Macrae showed that children's interpretations of sentences involving the directional prepositions *to/from*, *into/out of*, *on to/off* were affected by the way in which the interpretive task was presented to them. By varying the situation, she could get varying levels of apparent understanding.

The simplified argument about production and comprehension fails to take note of one fact which strongly favours production, in ordinary circumstances. When you produce language, you are in control: you need talk only about what you choose to talk about.

The point to be made is that we ordinarily speak within the flow of meaningful context which, as it were, supports – or at least does not conflict with – our language. It does not conflict with our language because we fit our utterances to its contours. The child's attention is drawn to something that interests him and he speaks of it. He has some idea that is important to him and he expresses it in whatever form comes most readily to him. He is never required, when he is himself producing language, to go counter to his own preferred reading of the situation – to the way in which he himself spontaneously sees it. But this is no longer necessarily true when he becomes the listener. And it is frequently not true when he is the listener in the formal situation of a psychological experiment – or indeed when he becomes a learner at school.

Lois Bloom reports some interesting findings obtained in work with a child called Peter, aged thirty-two months. Peter proved unable to imitate successfully a number of sentences which he had himself spontaneously produced the day before. Thus when Peter was asked, in the context of a game, to imitate 'I'm trying to get this cow in there' he produced only 'Cow in here'. And for 'You made him stand up there' he produced only 'Stand up there'. Lois Bloom concludes that the difficulty, in the imitation task, was that the sentences were not supported by any relation to immediate context and behaviour.

The findings of Dan Slobin and Charles Welsh are in line with Bloom's. They say that, if imitation is asked for almost immediately after the spontaneous production, it is likely to be more successful than if it is asked for even a few minutes later. Thus: 'If you finish your eggs all up, Daddy, you can have your coffee' is rendered again immediately as: 'After you finish your eggs all up then you can have your coffee, Daddy.' But if the original sentence is offered again for imitation after an interval of ten minutes, all the child manages to say is: 'You can have coffee, Daddy, after.'

Slobin and Welsh suggest that, in spontaneous speech, the child has an 'intention-to-say-so-and-so' – and that this intention sustains and supports the complex utterance. When the intention has faded and the child must process the utterance as pure isolated language the task for him is of a very different kind. This is fully in agreement with what has been argued here.

7. Disembedded Thought and Social Values

It is when we are dealing with people and things in the context of fairly immediate goals and intentions and familiar patterns of events that we feel most at home. And when we are asked to reason about these things, even verbally and at some remove from them, we can often do it well. So long as our thinking is sustained by this kind of human sense, and so long as the conclusion to which the reasoning leads is not in conflict with something which we know or believe or want to believe, we tend to have no difficulty. Thus even pre-school children can frequently reason well about the events in the stories they hear. However, when we move beyond the bounds of human sense there is dramatic difference. Thinking which does move beyond these bounds, so that it no longer operates within the supportive context of meaningful events, is often called 'formal' or 'abstract'. But these words are used in so many different ways that, to reduce the risk of confusion, they are perhaps best avoided here.* I shall speak rather of 'disembedded' thinking, hoping that the name will convey the notion that this is thought that has been prised out of the old primitive matrix within which originally all our thinking is contained.

Nevertheless, it is easy to see why the word 'formal' is often

---

* For instance, the kind of thinking I am talking about is not to be equated with what Piaget means by 'formal operational thought', still less with, say, the understanding of 'abstract notions' like 'hope' or 'justice'.

employed to refer to disembedded thought, for one way to move beyond the bounds of human sense is to express the *form* or logical structure of the reasoning in a way that leaves out content or meaning entirely. Let us see what is involved in this by considering the words (already quoted in Chapter 5) of the child who said:

> 'But how can it be [that they are getting married]? You have to have a man too!'

The underlying reasoning can evidently be restated thus:

> If there is a wedding there is a man involved.
> There is no man.
> Therefore there is no wedding.

Now let us look at the form or structure of this argument. To do so we have first to break the reasoning up into separate statements or propositions. Only two – together with the negations of these two – are involved here: *there is a wedding* and *there is a man*.

But these statements are loaded with meaning which we have to get rid of if we are to look at pure form. So let us replace the first of them – *there is a wedding* – by the symbol *p*; and let us replace the second one – *there is a man* – by the symbol *q*.

The reasoning then becomes:

> If *p*, then *q*.
> *Not q*.
> Therefore *not p*.

The striking fact is that, as soon as it is put thus, it becomes for many people mind-boggling. The human mind does not engage easily in the manipulation of meaningless symbols. Nial, at the age of only four, can reason easily about men and weddings. Most of us have to struggle when it comes to dealing with *p*s and *q*s.

Yet it is a fact not to be ignored that our kind of society places the highest value on a kind of thinking of which 'If *p*, then *q*. Not *q*, therefore not *p*' is a fairly extreme (though at the same time, elementary) example. The better you are at tackling problems without having to be sustained by human sense the more likely you are to succeed in our educational system, the more you will be approved of and loaded with prizes.

A number of years ago, when I was being taught the traditions and lore of intelligence-test construction, I asked the question: How are the items for these tests chosen? And I was told: We choose the ones which are best at predicting scholastic success. I then asked what determined which items would be 'good predictors' but no satisfactory answer seemed to be available. So I decided to look and see how these 'good predictors' were really working. When children fail, I wondered, why do they fail? What is it that they cannot do?

To try to find out, I sat down with some children between the ages of nine and thirteen and got them to tackle a selection of typical questions and talk to me about what they were doing. I asked them to 'think aloud' as far as possible.

It was revealing to find that many of the errors belonged to a category which I labelled 'arbitrary'. When an arbitrary error occurred the failure lay in the way the child's reasoning was related to the problem. He arrived at the wrong answer because he did not base his inferences strictly and firmly on the premises as they were stated. He imported new premises of his own – frequently basing them on human sense – or he ignored part of what was 'given'.

Now it is of the essence of these kinds of problem that you are required to stick strictly to the given. The problem is to be taken as encapsulated, isolated from the rest of existence. What you may judge to be important apart from it, what you may know to be true – these considerations are to be excluded. The thinking has to be disembedded. It is in the nature of the task that you must start from a limited set of premises or conditions and respect them strictly thereafter. Thus if you are given a problem about two boys called Pete and Tommy you are not supposed to introduce information about any real Pete or Tommy who happens to be known to you!

Children of five or six will often introduce such information freely. The more sophisticated child of nine upwards will seldom be quite so blatant, but he may still do what amounts to much the same thing. An instance is provided by a boy of twelve who chose the statement 'Tommy would wish his hair was red' as the conclusion from two premises postulating connection between red hair and the ability to play football well and gave as his reason 'because I would wish my hair was red'. In effect, this boy abandoned the given premises in favour of the alternative (unspoken) premise: 'All boys want to be good at football, just as I do.' He relied on human sense instead of asking himself what was compatible with the terms of the problem.

In a famous paper on the relationship between logic and thinking, Mary Henle describes how she asked a group of adult subjects to judge whether a set of conclusions could validly be drawn from the premises accompanying them. The subjects were asked to write down their judgements and the reasons for them; and they were told explicitly that they were to judge the logical adequacy of the conclusions, not their truth. But this they frequently failed to do.

Here is one of the problems, followed by two of the judgements that were made.

A group of women were discussing their household problems. Mrs Shivers broke the ice by saying: 'I'm so glad we're talking about these problems. It's so important to talk about things that are in our minds. We spend so much of our time in the kitchen that of course household problems are in our minds. So it is important to talk about them.' Does this follow?

One subject answered: 'No. Just because one spends so much time in the kitchen it does not necessarily follow that household problems are "in our minds".' But this answer is not a judgement on whether the conclusion ('So it is important to talk about them') is necessarily true *if* the premises are true. It is a rejection of one of the premises.

Another subject wrote: 'No. It is not important to talk about things that are in our minds unless they worry us, which is not the case.' This is a rejection of the other premise.

Mary Henle sees these answers as exemplifying what she calls 'failure to accept the logical task'. Other types of error involved completely overlooking one of the premises, inserting an extra premise, and restating a premise or a conclusion in such a way as to change the meaning.

What is particularly striking is that these subjects were graduate students at a university. We need not then be surprised if children find it difficult to reason from premises in a way which respects the premises strictly. And it is important to note that this is true even if the premises are not stated abstractly in terms of *p*s and *q*s. It is enough that they be somewhat controversial or liable to arouse emotional responses, or that they fail to 'make much sense'.

The work of Peter Wason and Philip Johnson-Laird provides another very interesting example of adult incapacity when reasoning unsupported by human sense is called for. They studied the ways in which sophisticated adult subjects (university undergraduates) dealt with the question of determining whether a rule was true. The rule had the form *if p, then q*, but Wason and Johnson-Laird did not use such fully abstract symbols. They did, however, use material which made very little sense in terms of everyday experience. The rule, as given to their subjects initially, was:

If a card has a vowel on one side, then it has an even number on the other side.

Four cards were presented, two of them showing letters of the alphabet (one consonant, one vowel), two of them showing numbers (one odd, one even), thus:

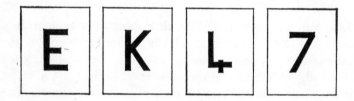

The subject was then told that his task was to 'name those cards, and only those cards, which need to be turned over in order to determine whether the rule is true or false.'

The correct answer is: the vowel and the odd number (E and 7) – *not* the even one (4).

This answer proves to be quite difficult for intelligent adults to appreciate – let alone to reach. But consider the following version of the task – which was used in a study by Johnson-

Laird, Legrenzi and Legrenzi – and bear in mind that it is the *same* task as regards logical structure.

The rule is now stated as follows:

If a letter is sealed then it has a five-penny stamp on it.

(This was in the days when there was one rate for sealed and one for unsealed mail.)

The accompanying material consists of four envelopes, thus:

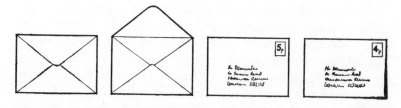

When the task was presented in this way it became relatively easy: 21 out of 24 subjects then knew that they had to turn over the sealed envelope (to make sure it had a five-penny stamp) *and* the letter with the four-penny stamp (to make sure it was not sealed). (Notice that the rule does not say that a letter bearing a five-penny stamp has to be sealed, so there is no need to turn this one over.) Of the same 24 subjects, only 2, by contrast, got the problem right when the rule was stated in a form that did not make 'human sense'.

As Wason and Johnson-Laird put it: 'The conditional rule, which proved so recalcitrant when its terms and conditions were arbitrary, has become almost trivially easy when it is embodied in a real task.'

There can be little doubt, then, that when we set such store by disembedded modes of thought we make the pursuit of education in our society a difficult enterprise for the human mind – one which many minds refuse at an early stage. To hark back to my study of intelligence-test items, one reason why many items were 'good predictors of scholastic success' was that children who relied on human sense and did not reason tightly from the premises got them wrong.

At this point it may be as well to emphasize that movement beyond the bounds of human sense is not an all-or-none affair. It is not a matter of taking a single step which makes us capable of efficient disembedded thinking thereafter in all circumstances. Thus a child who has begun to learn to tackle certain problems which have been 'prised out' from the supportive context of the rest of his experience is not thereby rendered instantly competent in the handling of formal systems of thought such as mathematics. And later in life it remains possible – indeed normal – to come to be at ease with some formal systems but not with others.

However, the argument here is that you cannot master *any* formal system unless you have learned to take at least some steps beyond the bounds of human sense, and that the problem of helping children to begin to do this in the early stages of their schooling—or even earlier—has not been properly recognized and is not usually tackled in any adequate way.

Thus we end up with a small number of educational 'successes' and a dismayingly large crop of 'failures'. And the urgent question is: how can this be avoided?

In principle, there are clearly two ways. We might change the value system – or we might find means to make the enterprise less daunting. We might teach the disembedded modes of thinking more successfully.

Changes in the value system could be of various kinds. The most obvious is a direct down-grading of the intellect—the sort of thing expressed commonly enough at the moment in such statements as 'Who cares about all that dry-as-dust stuff that has nothing to do with living?' But such 'anti-intellectual' statements certainly do not express the dominant values in the culture at the present time. And of course they are nonsense: the 'dry-as-dust stuff' has a great deal to do with life as we know it. For the paradox is that our most successful practical activities – our engineering, for example – would be impossible if we were to abandon the arduous task of functioning without the support of the world of familiar events. In order to handle the world with maximum competence it is necessary to consider the *structure* of things. It is necessary to become skilled in manipulating *systems* and in abstracting forms and patterns. This is a truth which, as a species, we have slowly come to know. If we were ever to renounce the activity, there would be a hefty price to pay.

However, we might change the value system without denying the significance of intellectual skills. We might simply reduce the relative weight we give to them, by substantially increasing the value we place on other things.

In some countries – China, for instance – serious attempts appear to have been made to do this. In our own country a certain amount of lip-service has been paid, but little has changed. The people who use their hands or their other talents in their work are most often people who have failed – or stubbornly refused in spite of considerable pressure – to meet the educational requirements for earning a living by the exercise of more or less intellectual capacities. This is true even where it is particularly evident that disembedded thinking needs to be allied to other kinds of competence.

Consider the engineering departments of our universities. They teach mathematics and physics – and so they should. But they do not teach people to make things. You can emerge as a graduate in mechanical engineering without ever having used a lathe or a milling-machine. *These* things are considered suitable only for the technicians. And for most of *them*, on the other hand, mathematics and physics beyond an elementary level are quite simply out of reach.

One of our greatest educational thinkers, Alfred North Whitehead, was deeply convinced that this *apartheid* is bad for all concerned. He expressed his misgivings in a brilliant essay on 'Technical education and its relation to science and literature', in which he laid it down as an educational axiom that 'in teaching you will come to grief as soon as you forget that your pupils have bodies', adding: 'It is a moot point whether the human hand created the human brain, or the brain created the hand. Certainly the connection is intimate and reciprocal.'

The paradoxical fact is that disembedded thinking, although by definition it calls for the ability to stand back from life, yields its greatest riches when it is conjoined with doing. Indeed, Whitehead thought that the separation of the two was likely to be disastrous for our civilization.

The separation is one that goes back to the beginnings of Western culture – even to the origins of literacy. Whitehead traces it to the Platonic ideal of a liberal education as an education for thought and for aesthetic appreciation where the only action contemplated is command. But we can go back further still to a most revealing Egyptian text, the original of which probably dates from around 2000 BC. The text is known as *The Satire on the Trades* and it consists of a father's exhortation to his son, as the son is being sent off to the Writing School to become a scribe. Here are a few extracts:

> I have seen how the belabored man is belabored – thou shouldst set thy heart in pursuit of writing. And I have observed how one may be rescued from his duties [sic!] – behold, there is nothing which surpasses writing . . .

> I have seen the metalworker at his work at the mouth of his furnace. His fingers were somewhat like crocodiles; he stank more than fish-roe . . .

> The small building contractor carries mud . . . He is dirtier than vines or pigs from treading under his mud. His clothes are stiff with clay . . .

> The arrow-maker, he is very miserable as he goes out into the desert [to get flint points]. Greater is that which he gives to his donkey than its work thereafter [is worth] . . .

> The laundry man launders on the [river] bank, a neighbour of the crocodile . . .

> Behold, there is no profession free of a boss—except for the scribe: he is the boss . . .

> Behold, there is no scribe who lacks food from the property of the House of the King – life, prosperity, health! . . . His father and his mother praise god, he being set upon the way of the living. Behold these things – I [have set them] before thee and thy children's children.

This document (which the children in the Writing Schools of the 19th Dynasty of Egypt were given as an exercise to copy, presumably so that they would get the right ideas) expresses vividly attitudes which are not at all unfamiliar today. But there can be no doubt that one reason for the continuing *apartheid* is that so many young people do not develop either aptitude or taste for the intellectual side of schooling.

The attempt to become skilled in the disembedded modes of intellectual activity is for most of us defeating or repugnant. (Of course, if it proves defeating it will inevitably be experienced as repugnant – of which more later.) If this were not so, we should not have a small, smug intellectual élite, convinced that this one attainment is enough to justify their whole existence and establish out-right their superiority.

So we turn now to the question of whether most children must inescapably fail to become competent in the exercise of disembedded thought. Are only a few of us *able* to learn to move beyond the bounds of human sense and function successfully there? I doubt it. While it may make some sense to postulate that we each possess some genetically determined 'intellectual potential', in which case individuals will surely differ in this respect as in others, there is no reason to suppose that most of us – or any of us for that matter – manage to come close to realizing what we are capable of. And it is not even certain that it makes a great deal of sense to think in terms of upper limits at all. For, as Jerome Bruner points out, there are tools of the mind as well as tools of the hand – and in either case the development of a powerful new tool brings with it the possibility of leaving old limitations behind. In a similar vein, David Olson says: 'Intelligence is not something we have that is immutable; it is something we cultivate by operating with a technology, or something we create by inventing new technology.'

The technology which Olson has particularly in mind is the system of making speech visible and permanent which we call writing.

8. Why Children Find School Learning Difficult

The arguments of the earlier chapters lead to a picture of the young human being in which the following are among the most prominent features.

1. First, he actively tries to make sense of the world from a very early point in his life: he asks questions, he wants to know. (This is evidently so as soon as verbal questions can be formulated. It is probably true even before language appears.) Also from a very early stage, the child has purposes and intentions: he wants to do. These questionings and these strivings imply some primitive sense of possibility which reaches beyond a realization of how things are to a realization of how they might be.

2. The sense of the possible which arises in conjunction with *wanting to know* involves, first, a simple realization of ignorance* ('There might be a tiger round the corner, I haven't

---

* But children do not always give evidence of knowing that they do not know. Sometimes they respond with apparent confidence when there is no way that they could know for sure – short of extra-sensory perception! Indeed this is one of the varieties of 'arbitrary error' – arbitrary because it involves neglecting some constraint in the problem – which I found in my earlier studies of children's thinking (see Donaldson, 1963); and more recently, Gilberte Piéraut-Le Bonniec has observed many other instances of the same kind of thing. When the colour of a hidden object was at issue she found that children between five and eight were liable simply to state what the colour was, showing no sign of uncertainty, no recognition of the distinction between a guess and a decision

looked') and then an attempt to use considerations of compatibility and incompatibility to extend the field of the known and reduce uncertainty. That which is possible then becomes that which does not lead to conflict with anything accepted as real or actual. Whatever does lead to such conflict is *impossible*. This is deductive inference. (But note that it does not become what is normally called *formal* deductive inference until attention centres not on conflict with the real in the known world, but on conflict with what we are accustomed to call 'the given', that is, with something merely postulated, something which you *decide* to accept as the premise on which you will base your reasoning. This is the distinction at issue in the studies of reasoning that were discussed in the last chapter. The 'formal' inference is disembedded.)

3. The sense of the possible which arises in conjunction with *wanting to do* involves, on the one hand, some apprehension of the goal, of the state of affairs which might be brought into being, and on the other hand some apprehension of the means, of the actions which one might take in order to reach the goal. However, it seems most probable that, in the early stages of life, awareness of the goal is dominant and that consideration of possible action – especially systematic consideration – comes later. There is a distinction to be drawn between trying different actions to achieve a goal and reflecting on these as a possible set of actions before performing them. This latter activity – the planning kind – involves the temporary suspension of overt action and a turning of attention inwards upon mental acts instead. Developmentally, the course of events is from an awareness of what is without to an awareness of what is within.

4. This is true also when we turn to the growth of linguistic skills. The child acquires these skills before he becomes aware of them. The child's awareness of what he talks *about* – the things out there to which the language refers – normally

---

based on firm information. These are curious findings. Yet there can be no doubt, on the other hand, that children much younger than these ages are *capable* of becoming aware of uncertainty. As soon as they spontaneously ask a genuine question it is quite clear that they have some sense of a gap in what they know.

takes precedence over his awareness of what he talks *with* – the words that he uses. And he becomes aware of what he talks with – the actual words – before he is at all aware of the rules which determine their sequencing – the rules which control his own production of them. (Indeed, a thoughtful adult has a very limited awareness of such processes in his own mind.)

In the early stages, before the child has developed a full awareness of language, language is embedded for him in the flow of the events which accompany it. So long as this is the case, the child does not interpret words in isolation – he interprets situations. He is more concerned to make sense of what people do when they talk and act than to decide what words mean. (After all he may not be aware of language, but he is keenly aware of other people.) But at the same time he is given to structuring, or making sense of, situations even when no words are uttered; and sometimes it seems that, when words *are* uttered, the child's interpretation of the utterance is strongly influenced by his own independent structuring of the context. If there is one feature of a situation which is salient for him – if it is the feature on which he himself would be most likely to comment – then this feature can exert a 'pull' on the interpretation of the words he hears. Just how powerful this pull may be is not yet entirely clear.

5. A child who is trying to figure out what other people mean must be capable of recognizing intentions in others, as well as having them himself. And such a child is by no means wholly unable to decentre. While he may certainly, like the rest of us, fail sometimes to appreciate the relativity of his own point of view, he is capable of escaping from it. Thus he is not debarred by egocentrism from communicating with us and relating to us in a personal way. Indeed personal relations appear to form the matrix within which his learning takes place.

If the picture which has just been sketched is accurate as to its main lines, the normal child comes to school with well-established skills as a thinker. But his thinking is *directed outwards* on to the real, meaningful, shifting, distracting world. What is going to be required for success in our educational system is that he should learn to turn language and thought in upon themselves. He must become able to direct his own thought processes in a thoughtful manner. He must become able not just to talk but to choose what he will say, not just to interpret but to weigh possible interpretations. His conceptual system must expand in the direction of increasing ability to represent itself. He must become capable of manipulating symbols.

Now the principal symbolic system to which the preschool child has access is oral language. So the first step is the step of conceptualizing language – becoming aware of it as a separate structure, freeing it from its embeddedness in events.*

Some children come to school with this step already taken – or at least with the movement already begun. They come with an enormous initial advantage.

Bärbel Inhelder and her colleagues have recently been trying to teach children to deal with Piagetian tasks such as class-inclusion. At one point in the book in which they report their findings they turn to the question of differences between children from different kinds of homes and whether linguistic skill is relevant. They go on to deny that 'language as such' has anything to do with success, but they say they have noticed certain differences in 'attitude' towards the words of the experimenter. Children from more privileged backgrounds are more likely to pay scrupulous attention to the words of the question, reflecting on them, analysing them before answering. By contrast, the less privileged children have a strong tendency to substitute a 'more natural' question for the one the experimenter has asked.†

* A very valuable survey of the available evidence about young children's awareness of language has recently been prepared by Eve Clark. She proposes that we recognize six types or levels of awareness, of which the simplest and earliest would be the monitoring of one's own speech (spontaneous corrections and the like) while the most complex – and latest to develop – would be reflection on the product of an utterance. She suggests that this last kind of awareness seems to call for skill in thinking about language structure in a way that is independent of language use.

† In a very recent paper, Robert Grieve and his colleagues confirm this. They observe that a young child is quite liable to 'amend

That there exist more or less 'natural' ways of describing certain situations or events is clear. Alison Macrae points out that an adult would be much more likely to say: 'The flowers are on top of the television set' than 'The television set is under the flowers'. And she reports that four-year-old children already appear to be sensitive to the oddity of the second version, for they tend to avoid using it even in a situation so constructed as to encourage its use. (There was incidentally no doubt about the ability of the children to produce the word 'under': they gave clear evidence of this in other contexts.)

Now to an unnatural statement there corresponds an unnatural question. If it is odd to say: 'The television set is under the flowers' then it is odd to ask 'Is the television set under the flowers?' Similarly, if it is odd to assert that there are more flowers than red flowers, it is odd to ask whether this is so.

The authors of the book on teaching children how to deal with Piagetian tasks – Bärbel Inhelder, Hermine Sinclair and Magali Bovet – make the remark about unnatural questions in passing; but it goes to the heart of the matter. The difference that they note amounts to a difference in readiness to treat language in some degree of abstraction from context. And it is easy to see how this would be encouraged in the more literate and intellectually sophisticated home.

As literate adults, we have become so accustomed to the written word that we seldom stop to think how dramatically it differs from the spoken one. The spoken word (unless recorded, which is another thing again) exists for a brief moment as one element in a tangle of shifting events – from which it must be disentangled if it is to be separately considered – and and then fades. The written word endures. It is there on the page, distinct, lasting. We may return to it tomorrow. By its very nature it can be quite free of non-linguistic context.* We

_____

our questions to ones more to his liking'; and they note the problems which this presents for the experimenter.

* Of course, illustrations in books provide non-linguistic contexts of a kind. Also much of the writing in our environment – the street sign, the soap packet, the TV advertisement – is heavily embedded in context. Some pre-school children appear to manage to teach themselves to read largely through their encounters with this kind of 'public print'. For an interesting discussion of children

can pick it up and slip it into a pocket or briefcase. Once a child has begun to learn to read he can bring his book home from school and read to his mother *the same words* which he read to his teacher in the class-room earlier in the day.

So a child's first encounters with books provide him with much more favourable opportunities for *becoming aware* of language in its own right than his earlier encounters with the spoken word are likely to have done.

Of course in some homes awareness of the spoken word is greatly encouraged. Some parents talk *about* words to their children, play word games with them and so on. But most talk only *with* words. Indeed, a great many children come to school not even aware that separate words exist – that the flow of speech can be broken up into these units. It is true, as Fox and Routh have recently shown, that by the age of four children are not incapable of breaking speech up into progressively smaller 'little bits' if encouraged to do so. However, it is certain that many of them will never have thought of doing so. Also many five-year-olds have very confused notions of what is meant by the word 'word', as Jess Reid showed in a highly original study of the conceptions of the reading process which children bring with them to school and which they develop as the first year at school goes on. These findings have since been confirmed and extended by John Downing.

For many children the earliest encounter with the written word is indirect, arising in the situation where a story is read aloud by an adult. This is already in a sense language freed from context; but the experience of hearing a story is not so likely to enhance awareness as the direct grappling with words on a page (for reasons to which we shall return). It is a striking fact that when young children listen to stories they very seldom ask questions about the language in which the stories are told. They ask many searching questions about the intentions and motives of the characters, the structure of the plot – if you like, the meaning of the story. They rarely ask about the meanings of the words, even when these must clearly be unfamiliar.

---

who read before they enter school see Margaret Clark's book, *Young Fluent Readers*.

In the set of story-time recordings of children's speech which were quoted in Chapter 4 (and which were collected daily over a period of roughly four months) one can find only three examples of questions about word meanings and only one about any other aspect of language.

The three questions about word meanings are:

'What's a "howdah"?'
'What is "cud"?' and
'What's "mousey quiet"? Excuse me, what's "mousey quiet"?'

The first two of these questions were from a child of almost five, who was already learning to read although not yet at school and who showed great interest in print whenever she could lay hands on it. The third question was again from a child who was nearly five years old, and who, though she had not begun to read, came from a highly literate home.

The one remaining question about language was asked by a child not quite three. The story-teller read the sentence: 'And at last they *did* pull up the turnip.' The child asked in a very high and excited voice: 'Why is it *did*?' This appears to be a question about grammatical structure (one which, incidentally, the story-teller found very hard to answer), but it is quite isolated. Nothing else of the kind occurred at all.

Now it is not that young children are incapable of asking *any* question about the relation between words and things. One of the very earliest questions commonly recorded in a child's speech is: 'What dat?' This is frequent at the first stage of language production, commonly reached before the age of two, and it appears to be a request to know an object's name. So it seems strange that the request to know what a word means – a question dealing with the same relation but starting from the opposite end – should be so much slower to come.

It is not, however, clear that the child's early request for a name is quite what it appears to be. There are reasons for suspecting that to a young child the name of an object may be on a par, say, with the object's weight or with its colour – just an attribute among other attributes, hence more like a part of the object than a part of some separate formal system called 'language'. Vygotsky has argued powerfully in support of this interpretation, pointing out that for intellectually unsophisticated adults the same may also to some extent be true. He tells the story of the peasant who was not so much surprised that it had been possible to figure out how big the stars are as that it had been possible to discover their names.

So a request for a name does not by itself prove that language is apprehended as a distinct system. It seems that, in general, this apprehension is slow to come and that one effect of learning to read may be to encourage the conscious reflection which produces it. Vygotsky's peasant must surely have been illiterate.

It is clear that being aware of language as a distinct system is relevant to the business of separating what is *said* from what is done or from what is somehow salient in a situation – and hence to dealing successfully with Piagetian tests like conservation or class-inclusion and with many other reasoning tasks. As Inhelder and her colleagues have pointed out, some children take stock of what precisely the experimenter has asked them, while others substitute a 'more natural question' of their own.

However, while it is evident that this last strategy can hardly work, we must be cautious about drawing the conclusion that some degree of reflective awareness of language is all that success requires. For there would also seem to be, at the very least, the issue of *control* – the question of how much ability the child has to sustain attention, resisting irrelevance while he considers implications. And young children seem not to be very good at this. For instance, Lesley Hall carried out experiments in which she asked her subjects to decide whether statements were true or false in relation to pictures and then recorded eye movements as the subjects searched the pictures and reached a decision. She found that children as young as four could organize their search patterns to some extent if no irrelevant pictures were shown but that the presence of irrelevant pictures was 'more efficacious in "attracting" the gaze than was any cognitive plan in "projecting" it.' In other words, the amount of deliberate control which the children exercised in this context appeared to be quite limited. This question of control is at the heart of the capacity for disembedded thinking which, as we have seen, involves sticking to the problem and refusing to be diverted by knowledge, by beliefs or by perceptions which have nothing to do with it.

Yet it turns out that recognition of the importance of being able to control one's own thinking may not take us so very far from the issue of awareness after all. What is now at stake, however, is the child's more general awareness of his own thought processes – his *self-awareness*. For as Vygotsky rightly says: '. . . control of a function is the counterpart of one's consciousness of it.' If a child is going to control and direct his own thinking, in the kind of way we have been considering, he must become conscious of it.

We are still not well-informed about how self-awareness grows. But Piaget has recently reported the results of a very interesting series of studies (see *The Grasp of Consciousness*).

The method used was to give children a number of tasks to perform and get them to talk about their own actions. The tasks might be very simple ones, presenting no difficulty at all for the children, such as crawling on hands and knees. Or they might be problems of some complexity like the Tower of Hanoi puzzle. (In this puzzle there are three sticks, one of which has on it a number of discs varying in size, with the biggest at the bottom. The problem then is to move these discs to one of the other sticks, moving only one at a time and never putting a larger disc on top of a smaller one.)

Piaget's findings and arguments are complex, but one point that emerges very clearly is that awareness typically develops when something gives us pause and when consequently, instead of just acting, we stop to consider the possibilities of acting which are before us. The claim is that we heighten our awareness of what is actual by considering what is possible. We are conscious of what we do to the extent that we are conscious also of what we do *not* do – of what we might have done. The notion of *choice* is thus central.

So what makes us stop and think about our thinking – and thus makes us able to *choose* to direct our thinking in one way rather than another? We cannot expect to find any simple answer to such a momentous question – but observe how, here again, learning to read may have a highly significant contribution to make. The child who is learning to read is in a situation that is likely to encourage him to begin to consider possibilities in relation to at least one important act of thought: the apprehension of meaning. As one child put it: 'You have to stop and think. It's difficult!' Here the same arguments apply as were relevant to the growth of awareness of language itself: the critical things are that the written word is enduring, and that it can be free of non-linguistic context. Thus non-linguistic context does not here act – as it so often does with the spoken word – to determine one interpretation, shaping the meaning and excluding the need for choice; and further, the lasting character of the print means that there is time to stop and think, so that the child has a chance to consider possibilities – a chance of a kind which he may never have had before.

Thus it turns out that those very features of the written word which encourage awareness of language may also encourage awareness of one's own thinking and be relevant to the development of intellectual self-control, with incalculable consequences for the development of the kinds of thinking which are characteristic of logic, mathematics and the sciences.

9. What the School Can Do

It is universally recognized that, when children come to school, there is a wide gap between those who are best prepared and those who are least prepared for school learning. The question then is how to close the gap *early*, for if it is not soon closed it will widen. This is the way with gaps of such a kind.

Some would say that when children reach school it is already too late – or that nothing can be done without direct intervention in the homes of the 'underprivileged'. I do not believe, however, that their arguments are conclusive (which is not at all to say that I question the value of efforts at the pre-school stage or with the children's parents).

The rest of this chapter is concerned with what can be done to give *all* children a good start in the kind of learning that takes place in school. But some children need more help than others in making this good start, so that for them what the teacher does can potentially make a greater difference.

For reasons which have been discussed in the last chapter, I believe that the early mastery of reading is even more important than it is commonly taken to be.

And here the first thing is to recognize how great may be the *conceptual* problems which the child encounters in the beginning, especially if his home has not prepared him adequately. He may in the first place, as we have seen, have little reflective awareness of the spoken language even though he can use language competently in everyday situations. He may in the second place have no clear idea at all about what kind of activity this thing called 'reading' *is*. Jess Reid has shown that some children, even after three or four months in school, cannot say how the postman knows which house to bring a letter to or how their mothers know which bus to take. And they do not really have any understanding of what an adult is doing when he holds a newspaper in front of his face and says to them: 'Now you be quiet!'

So the preparation for reading should include, as a most important component, attempts to make children more aware of the spoken tongue. It is not just a matter of helping them to use speech more effectively, it is a matter of helping them to notice what they are doing. For instance, many of them will never before have realized that the flow of speech, which they have been producing and interpreting unreflectingly for years, is composed of *words*. Yet this realization is indispensable if they are to deal sensibly with the grouped and spaced marks on paper which, as they must now come to see, correspond to the spoken language. Awareness of this correspondence – even of its existence, much less of its nature – should never be taken for granted. It is essential to make certain that the child understands that the marks on paper are a written version of speech. And it is important thereafter to help him to recognize the special functions and usefulness of this written version – as an aid to memory, as a means of communicating at a distance and so on. If these preliminaries are well taken care of, then he will see the sense and purpose of what he is about to do and will be rescued from the bewilderment of struggling to master an activity the nature of which he does not comprehend.

Once the teaching of reading is begun, the manner in which it is taught may be of far-reaching significance. We all know that the attainment of literacy is of great practical importance for life in our society. But, if the arguments of the preceding chapters are sound, then the *process* of becoming literate can have marked – but commonly unsuspected – effects on the growth of the mind. It can do this by encouraging highly important forms of intellectual self-awareness and self-control.

It is at once evident that different ways of teaching reading may be expected to do this to differing degrees. A key consideration will be whether the child is given time to pause. In later life, great value is often placed on 'rapid reading' and it is obviously useful for an adult to be able to read fast when he has to. But speed and reflective thought are antithetical at any age. I. A. Richards, stressing the importance of the latter, wrote a whole book on *How to Read a Page*.

If one wants to encourage the development of reflective skills in the early stages, then speed and certainty will *not* be the things to stress. The child who is expected to respond by immediately making the right sound whenever an isolated word is shot at him on what is known as a 'flash card' will not be considering possibilities of interpretation at all. If he does not know, he will be under pressure to guess wildly, not to pause and reflect and become aware of what he is doing.

Moreover, the 'flash card' technique not only tends to deprive the child of time – it deprives him of another prerequisite for the thoughtful consideration of possibilities. For this can take place only when there is a situation with enough structure in it to reduce the possibilities to some manageable set. Time alone is not enough. No one, child or adult, can weigh up possibilities in a situation where they are infinite – or even very numerous. Now although words on a page are free of non-linguistic context (apart from illustrations), they normally occur in a linguistic one: they occur in meaningful sentences and paragraphs. And it is this context which can be used to provide the structure.

A child will have the best chance of starting to consider possibilities of meaning if he is reading a coherent text which contains the right sort of balance between words he already knows well and words he is not sure about and if, further, the known and familiar parts of the text are so constructed as to guide him towards a manageable set of options when the unknown is encountered.

This brings with it yet another requirement: the grammatical structure of the text must not be too alien to the grammatical forms of the child's speech. The written word differs from the spoken word in ways we have not yet considered. Its development over the centuries has entailed the elaboration of literary forms – inversions, literary idioms, stylistic devices of many kinds – which have carved a great gulf between the language we speak and the language we write. For instance, we might write: 'Whom should he see but the old woman.' We would not be at all likely to say it.

Children must learn to master the literary forms. But they will learn best to grapple with possibilities of meaning if they are allowed to deal *in the beginning* with the familiar cadences of the spoken tongue.* Thereafter the literary forms should be introduced gradually as the child's competence – and confidence – grow.

I am indebted to Jess Reid for many discussions which have helped me to see these things more clearly. Her reading programme, *Link-up*, written with Joan Low, is the only one I know which takes them fully into account.

The hope, then, is that reading can be taught in such a way as greatly to enhance the child's reflective awareness, not only of language as a symbolic system but of the processes of his own mind. Important as reading is, however, there is no reason to suppose it is the only way. As Vygotsky put it: 'All the higher functions have in common awareness, abstraction and control.' And he believed that all of the school subjects could be made to contribute to the growth of 'consciousness and deliberate mastery', which he called 'the principal contributions of the school years'. But again of course much will depend on the manner of the teaching. For instance, if the child is taught to operate with the decimal system without coming to understand that it is one system among other possible ones then, to quote Vygotsky once more, 'he has not mastered the system but is, on the contrary, bound by it.'

Of course, such liberating understanding is the final outcome, not the starting point. You cannot begin the teaching of arithmetic with a lecture on the concept of a numerical base. But from the beginning you can be conscious of working

* I believe this to be true even for children who, because of years of listening to stories read to them at home, already have some familiarity with the structure of the language we write as distinct from the language we speak. It is all the more true for those who have lacked this experience or have had it only to a limited degree. For the latter, it is of the highest importance that they should have stories read to them in school, and that these should be chosen for the qualities of the language as well as the merits of the story.

99

towards such an end. And from the beginning you can try to help the child towards some degree of understanding of the general nature of the learning activity that he is about to engage in, so that, before he gets down to the confusion of the detail, he has at least a rudimentary sense of the kind of thing he is attempting.

This has already been illustrated for the case of reading. It applies equally to all subjects. But it is as well to recognize that the giving of this first vital glimpse of a subject matter to a young child is not easy.* For one thing, it makes great demands on the teacher's capacity for decentring (see Chapter 2). An adult's knowledge of the general nature of the subjects taught to children when they first enter school is apt to be so well established that it blocks the realization of precisely what the children need to be helped to see.

It is the same with the giving of instructions. The example provided by Laurie Lee (see Chapter 2) should be a vivid reminder of the hazards. It is never easy to give 'self-sufficient' instructions to young children. Often the instructions cannot be correctly interpreted without information which the instruction itself does not provide and which the child may lack. The younger the child and the greater the gulf between the culture of the school and the culture of his home, then the greater is the risk. For instance, if you tell a child to 'look at the picture which *comes after* this one' when he is not familiar with the conventions that govern the way we order things on a page, he will not be able to comply. Is he then to be judged stupid?

It is not possible for a teacher, however sensitive and imaginative, and well-informed, to anticipate fully all the difficulties of this kind that will arise. So we must ask whether we could do more to get children to tell us when they do not understand and to ask us for more information. Peter Lloyd found in the studies described in Chapter 2 that pre-school

---

* Nor is it only young children who may need this kind of help. A student who had been highly proficient in mathematics at school but who had learned almost no physics reports having experienced considerable difficulty in the early stages of studying physics at university because of a failure to understand the type of difference that exists between mathematics and a physical science.

children would seldom spontaneously ask for information when they had received an inadequate message but that they could often do this after explicit encouragement. Such 'learning to ask' should be of direct value in itself, for it implies that the child become conscious of his uncertainty over the interpretation of what the teacher says. Thus his self-awareness will grow.

In their willingness to give expression to their puzzlement children, of course, differ greatly. In spite of Peter Lloyd's general observation, I vividly recall one nursery school child who seemed never to let anything pass without the most searching interrogation of any adult who was available for questioning. Individual differences will always be with us.

For the teacher, the most prominent individual difference is apt to lie in the ease with which children can be helped to achieve new learning. Vygotsky argued that it is educationally more informative to know what a child can do with 'some slight assistance' than to know what he succeeds at unaided. Two children may be equal in what they can do on their own but not equally easy to help, as every teacher knows. One way to look at this is to say that the one who is hard to help is not 'ready to learn' – and then to leave him alone until, with luck, he becomes ready. Another way is to say that the one who is hard to help is the one who needs help more – and then to try to find out precisely what he needs, where his present deficits lie. For, as Bruner says, to be 'ready' to learn a given skill is precisely to be already equipped with other prerequisite skills.

The essence of the teacher's art lies in deciding what help is needed in any given instance and how this help may best be offered; and it is clear that for this there can be no general formula. Yet perhaps it is possible to say something useful about the *kinds* of help that are likely to be of value. A recent paper by Robert Siegler bears on this question.

The problem which Siegler studied was the familiar 'balance-scale' problem: how to predict which side of a simple balance beam will go down when given weights are placed on given pegs.

Siegler took some children aged five and some children aged eight who initially seemed to tackle problems of this kind in exactly the same way. Then he gave all the children experience with what he called 'conflict problems' – that is, problems where on one side of the beam there were more weights but the weights·were at a lesser distance from the fulcrum (e.g. 4 weights on peg 2), while on the other side there were fewer weights but they were at a greater distance (e.g. 3 weights on peg 3). This meant that attention to weight alone would yield one prediction while attention to distance alone would yield another. What then emerged was that the eight-year-olds tended to profit from experience with the conflict problems and to develop more advanced and adequate rules; while the five-year-olds appeared to be affected not at all.

So one might say that the five-year-olds were not 'ready' to learn, at least in this way. This, however, explains nothing. Why did these children not learn? Siegler went on to try to find out.

His conclusion was that the difference lay in the way the children 'encoded' the problem, or represented it to themselves. It was a question of precisely what they attended to – or noted – in the problem's structure.

Siegler used two ways of determining what the children were encoding when they looked at a balance beam at the start of a problem. First he made individual observations of a number of children as they tackled the problems, asking them questions and noting their comments. Next he showed the children various configurations of weights on different pegs but instead of asking for a prediction he asked the children to take a good look and then to construct the same configuration on another balance beam after the first one had been removed. The value of this reproductive procedure was that it yielded evidence about what the child was noticing that was independent of his skill at making successful predictions.

By these means, Siegler showed that the five-year-olds commonly took note of the number of weights on each side of the balance but they ignored the distance of these weights from the fulcrum.

The question then was why the younger children encoded distance less effectively than weight – and what could be done about it. Siegler tried to find out. He asked, for instance, whether they simply needed more time but found that that was not the answer. He tried the effect of simply telling the children what to encode, but this left the age difference still intact. Finally he gave very explicit instructions and practice in copying configurations. 'You do it like this. First you count the number of weights on this side – one, two, three, four. Then you count the number of pegs the weights are from the centre – one, two, three. So you say to yourself "four weights on the third peg",' – and so on.

After this there followed demonstrations by the experimenter, the joint tackling of a copying problem by child and experimenter, and seven practice trials by the child with the experimenter by his side to tell him if he went wrong.

Finally, the five-year-olds who had been taught to represent the configurations in this way took part in an experiment in which they were given the same experience with prediction problems of the 'conflict' kind that had previously produced no apparent learning in their age-mates. And now a different result was obtained: the five-year-olds, like the eight-year-olds, were able to profit from the experience and learn to solve the prediction problems more successfully. They still did not gain as much as the eight-year-olds but they made substantially more progress than before. They were more ready to learn.

It is by no means certain how widely we can generalize Siegler's results, but it seems likely that he has demonstrated something that is pervasive. If you want to solve a problem it is obviously desirable, to say the least, that you should be able to register those features which are relevant to the solution. Also there may be better or worse ways of representing these features – ways that make them more or less easy to remember and to manage in the mind.* And so a large part of the teacher's task may be to help children to achieve efficient inner representations of the problem they are expected to tackle.

Thus the conclusion to Siegler's investigation of 'readiness' lends further endorsement to the idea that it is important to help a child to have a proper understanding of the nature of the learning tasks that he embarks on. But earlier, when this notion was emphasized, we were considering understanding on a very general level: what *are* these activities of reading, or

* Some striking illustrations of this are given by Bruner in *Toward a Theory of Instruction*, Chapter 3.

counting or whatever, and what are they for? Now we are talking rather about the importance of achieving a more detailed representation of task structure. It is easy to illustrate this by reference to reading once again.

While, at the most general introductory level, the child needs to understand that these marks that he sees on paper correspond, in some way still unspecified, to the spoken language, his later task is to figure out the details of this correspondence. Yet between the extreme generality of understanding that there *is* correspondence and the extreme detail of learning what each configuration of letters stands for, there arises the intermediate question: what kind of correspondence is it?

The most obvious hypothesis for a child to entertain concerning the answer to this question is that the correspondence is of a one-to-one kind. That is, once he realizes that written words are composed of letters and spoken words of sounds, he is most likely to suppose initially that each letter corresponds to ('stands for' or 'says') one and only one sound.

This, as we know, is untrue. And if a child believes that the relationship has this kind of structure he will soon be in very serious difficulty. Yet teachers often systematically encourage him to believe just this falsehood which he is so ready to accept. They teach him that the letter *e* corresponds to the sound / ɛ /, as in *hen*, although it is plain that he cannot progress any way at all as a reader without encountering words like *he* and *me*.

It is true that the false general rule is often quickly followed by others which are aimed at amending it, such as the one about 'magic *e* at the end of a word which makes the vowel say its name.' But although there is the word *here*, there are also, alas, the words *there* and *were*!

The question then is whether the true nature of the correspondence between the units of the written English language and those of the spoken English language should not be made clear to a child almost from the moment when he first starts to look at written words analytically, with attention to letters and letter order. The truth is that for most letters – and for certain letter groups – there exists a set of options in the sound system. The correspondence is not one-to-one, it is one-to-n – that is, one-to-two, or -three or more.* Thus the letter c can be pronounced as in *c*andle or it can be pronounced as in i*c*ing.

It seems to be widely believed that children must not be told the truth about the system to begin with because they could not cope with such complexities. I believe this to be quite mistaken. What underlies the mistake is, I think, a failure to make a crucial distinction – a failure to see the difference between understanding the nature of the system and mastering all the individual patterns of relationship. It will inevitably take a child some time to learn all the sets of correspondences. The question is simply whether he will do this better if he is correctly informed about the kind of thing to expect.

There is no reason to suppose that children of five cannot understand a system that contains options. We have already seen that from an early age they have some sense of situations where more than one possibility is open. They know very well that you can either walk or cycle or go by car. They know very well that if someone is not at school he may either have measles or have a cold or. be playing truant. And Barbara Wallington has shown that at least from the age of three-and-a-half they can understand and operate with such statements as 'the little house is either in that box or in that box'.

Young children are not likely spontaneously to formulate hypotheses that specify alternatives – but that is another matter. All the more reason why, if the system they are dealing with does involve options, we should tell them so.† They will

---

* There is also, of course, a set of correspondences in the opposite direction – that is, from the sounds to the written symbols. Thus, a given sound may be represented in more than one way – e.g., /k/ by the letter k or the letter c or the letters ck. But these sound-to-written-symbol relationships are relevant for spelling, not for reading. It is obviously of great importance that the child should be helped to avoid confusion over this. At present such help is frequently not given.

† Support for this view is given by Gibson and Levin in their authoritative book *The Psychology of Reading*. They conclude that: 'The nature of the correspondence system should be revealed as soon as possible if transfer is to be optimized.' (Page 73.)

then understand the *sort of thing* they have to learn. This way of proceeding would not only appear to offer the best hope of mastering word decoding skills. It must have the further general advantage – if the whole argument of this book is well-founded – of encouraging reflective thought and awareness of the processes of the mind.

Children, even quite young ones, will not let themselves be passively led. They will actively invent and discover, using what we tell them as a starting point. But we must try not to hinder them by putting them down at starting points from which the road is unnecessarily long and hard. I am reminded of the story of the man who, when asked how to get to Little Boglington, answered: 'If I was you, I wouldn't start from here.'

Lauren Resnick, writing of her studies in the teaching of mathematics, urges that we should not underestimate the strength of the child's tendency to engage in active invention. She argues that we are 'not faced so much with a choice between teaching by rules and teaching by discovery as with a problem of finding teaching rules that will enhance the probability of discovery.' And she stresses that rules which are to have any chance of meeting this requirement must never be rules which obscure the structure of the task.

However, no matter how skilled we become at displaying the structure of a given task and helping the child to represent it to himself efficiently, we must not deceive ourselves. The learner, if he is an active discoverer, will make mistakes. So it is as well to reflect a little on the role of error in the learning process and what we should do about it.

According to some educational theories, it is not a good thing ever to be wrong, and it is an important part of the teacher's function to keep his pupils from error, planning every step of the way, so that they avoid pitfalls.

This sort of educational notion tends to go along with a belief that the mainspring of learning is reward or punishment administered from without. On this view, learning occurs when correct responses are 'stamped in' and when wrong ones are 'stamped out' – that is all there is to it. The best thing, then, may seem to be to prevent the wrong ones from ever occurring.

There are no doubt certain types of learning situation where something like this does happen and where mistakes are better avoided. But it is also quite clear that error can play a highly constructive role in the development of thinking. It is now well established that the advent of error can be a sign of progress (which, of course, is not to say that all error is to be interpreted in this way). It turns out that the following sequence is commonly observed to occur: first the child tackles something correctly, then he starts to make systematic errors, then he returns to what appears on the surface to be his original correct response.

Many examples can be given, but one provided in a recent paper by Annette Karmiloff-Smith and Bärbel Inhelder is in some ways particularly interesting.

The task for the children was to balance a set of blocks across a narrow beam. Sometimes the blocks had their weight evenly distributed along their length so that the centre of gravity and the geometric centre coincided, sometimes they were more heavily weighted at one end. When the weight was not symmetrical, the differences between the ends might or might not be visible: sometimes the blocks were weighted with metal hidden inside them.

On this task the youngest subjects were often successful in situations where older ones failed and still older ones succeeded. What seemed to happen was that the very young children were guided almost entirely by the 'feel' of the blocks: they had no kind of theory. They took each block in turn and simply balanced it. But primitive theories – 'theories-in-action' the authors call them – soon appeared on the scene. The children began to try to operate systematically and according to rules. Notice that this was not a teaching study – the children evolved the rules spontaneously.

Of course it often happened that the children did not state the rules that they were using, though remarks like: 'Things always balance in the middle' were recorded. Even without such explicit formulations, however, the 'existence' of rules can be inferred from observation of behaviour, just as the operation of some sorts of grammatical rule is inferred from the speech of children long before they could themselves give any account of what these rules are.

This is the kind of thing that was observed to happen: the

children at the intermediate stage would lift an asymmetrically weighted block and, apparently ignoring the 'feel', would place it down across the bar at the mid-point of its length. It would fall off. They would try again, doing exactly the same thing – and of course it would fall again. But sometimes the 'mid-point' rule would work because for some of the blocks the weight was equally distributed. This partial success seemed to be enough to keep the theory alive for some time. It was as if the child had to consolidate his first theory before he could modify it so as to deal with counter-examples. And then the modified theory would tend to grow up alongside the original one, instead of ousting it suddenly.

It is not surprising if, when rules are first devised for dealing with a complex system, they should be inadequate and oversimplified,* so that their application leads to error in certain cases. What is of interest is the manner in which the inadequate rules are replaced by better ones and the errors transcended.

In the case we have been considering, the situation was such that the child could clearly see that his theory was wrong. Sometimes it is not so obvious – and being wrong without knowing it is clearly not of much value! So if we are going to try to put the occurrence of error to good use in education, we must ask how we can make children aware of their errors – how we can help to bring them to the critical realization: 'I am wrong!'†

There is a very famous historical example of this being done by a great teacher. In the dialogue called the *Meno*, Plato describes how Socrates gave a slave boy a lesson in geometry.

---

* The fact that the hypotheses which the child evolves for himself are often at first oversimplified might be used as an argument for presenting him with oversimplified rules on the grounds that this somehow 'follows nature'. But in my opinion this argument is highly suspect. What the child works out for himself has a quite different status in his mind from what he is told by an authoritative adult. It is one thing to turn to good educational use errors that spontaneously arise. It is quite another to introduce them.

† We must also ask how we can help the child to face and overcome his own errors without feeling defeated and withdrawing from the learning task – but of that more later (see Chapter 10).

The slave boy came to the lesson with the false belief that if you doubled the area of a square you thereby doubled the length of its sides. Thus, if a square, 2 feet by 2 feet, has an area of 4 square feet, then another square of twice the area, namely 8 square feet, will have sides of twice the length, namely 4 feet.

Socrates proceeds, by a succession of questions, to lead the slave boy into self-contradiction. The boy then acknowledges that his original belief was wrong and that he does not know how long the sides of the new square will have to be if the area is to be double. When this point in the lesson is reached, Socrates makes the following comment:

> At the beginning he did not know the side of the square of 8 (square) feet. Nor indeed does he know it now, but then he thought he knew it and answered boldly as was appropriate – he felt no perplexity. Now however he does feel perplexed. Not only does he not know the answer – he doesn't even think he knows.

In other words, the slave boy is now *aware* of his error. Socrates goes on to argue that, by perplexing the boy, he has put him in a stronger position for now the boy will want to know. So long as he thought he knew, there was clearly no hope of change, for he was satisfied with his state. But he cannot be satisfied with a state of ignorance and confusion. He will want to get himself out of it.

The former of these two assertions can scarcely be challenged. But what about the latter? *Will* he want to get himself out of it? Or will he merely be discouraged and give up?

What makes us want to learn?

10. The Desire to Learn

At a very early age, human babies show signs of a strong urge to master the environment. They are limited in what they can do by the slow development of their skill in controlling their own movements. Thus it is fair to call them 'helpless' in the sense that they cannot manage the environment well enough to survive unaided. This makes it all the more interesting to discover that the urge to manage the environment is already there at this time of helplessness and that it does not appear to derive from anything else or to depend on any reward apart from the achieving of competence and control.

For some time past it has been widely accepted that babies – and other creatures – learn to do things because certain acts lead to 'rewards'; and there is no reason to doubt that this is true. But it used also to be widely believed that effective rewards, at least in the early stages, had to be directly related to such basic physiological 'drives' as thirst or hunger. In other words, a baby would learn if he got food or drink or some sort of physical comfort, not otherwise.

It is now clear that this is not so. Babies will learn to behave in ways that produce results in the world with no reward except the successful outcome. For an example of work which shows this clearly we may turn to some studies carried out by Hanus Papoušek.

Papoušek began by using milk in the normal way to 'reward' the babies he studied and so teach them to carry out some simple movements, such as turning the head to one side or the other. Then he noticed that an infant who had had enough to drink would refuse the milk but would still go on making the learned response with clear signs of pleasure. So he began to study the children's responses in situations where no milk was provided. He quickly found that children as young as four months would learn to turn their heads to right or left if the movement 'switched on' a display of lights – and indeed that they were capable of learning quite complex sequences of head turns to bring about this result. For instance, they could learn to make alternating turns to left and right; or to make double alternating turns (two left, two right); or to make as many as three consecutive turns to one side.

Papoušek's light display was placed directly in front of the infants and he made the interesting observation that sometimes they would not turn back to watch the lights closely although they would 'smile and bubble' when the display came on. Papoušek concluded that it was not primarily the sight of the lights which pleased them, it was the success they were achieving in solving the problem, in mastering the skill. If he is right in this – and there is a considerable amount of other confirming evidence – then we may conclude that there exists a fundamental human urge to make sense of the world and bring it under deliberate control.

Papoušek argues further that what his babies are doing as they try to achieve this control is matching incoming information about the world against some sort of inner 'standard'. And this amounts to saying that they are already engaged in building some kind of 'model' of bits of the world – some mental representation of what it is like. They then experience satisfaction when the fit between the model and the world is good, dissatisfaction when it is bad – that is, when the expected result fails to occur, when the lights do not go on. Papoušek reports 'increased tension and finally upsetness and signs of displeasure' in the latter case.

Now on even the simplest notion of what is involved in adaptation, it can come as no surprise that dissatisfaction arises when prediction fails. As soon as a species abandons reliance on instinctual patterns of behaviour and begins to rely instead on building inner representations and making predictions then it becomes critical for survival to get the predictions right. Thus the realization of incongruity between our notion of the world and what it turns out to be like should naturally lead us to want to understand it better. And many different theories about the growth of intelligent thought stress that this kind of cognitive conflict is unacceptable to us, that it is something we try to get rid of. After the early stages, the conflict may be between different parts of our world model. If we come to face the fact that we hold two inconsistent beliefs we find this uncomfortable. And so we should. For it is axiomatic that the different parts of a model must fit together.

This argument obviously harks back to what was said in the last chapter about the educational value of becoming aware of error. But there are two further considerations which now need to be added. Firstly, it is not only when incongruities are forced on us by events that we try to resolve them. Sometimes we positively seek them out, as if we liked having to deal with things that we do not understand, things that challenge us intellectually. But secondly we may, on the contrary, become afraid of meeting incongruity, afraid of realizing that we are wrong, and we may then take steps to defend ourselves against this recognition by avoiding situations that are likely to give rise to it. We may withdraw.

These are sharply contrasted responses and the difference between them is of crucial educational importance. Education should aim to encourage the readiness to come to grips with incongruity and even to seek it out in a positive fashion, enjoying challenge. Equally, it should aim to discourage defence and withdrawal. But often it seems in effect to do exactly the opposite. The reasons for this cannot become clear without consideration of another topic: the development of the self-image.

We are beings who ask questions; we are beings who make value judgements, holding some things good and important, others bad or worthless; and we are beings who build models of the world. In the course of time, these models come to include some representation of ourselves as part of the world. It is thus inevitable that we should arrive at the question: of what value am I? And it is also inevitable that the answer should matter to us a great deal.

When a child first asks this question, how is he to get the answer? One obvious way will be to try to discover what value other people place upon him. With increasing maturity, when he has perhaps managed to develop a more independent value system of his own, the judgements of others may come to matter less. But while he is still a young child they are bound to exert powerful influence on his self-esteem.

I have been arguing that there is a fundamental human urge to be effective, competent and independent, to understand the world and to act with skill. I am reminded of a little girl of eighteen months, verbally somewhat precocious, who, when she was offered help with anything, was given to saying firmly: 'Can man'ge.' To this basic urge to 'manage' there is added in our kind of culture very strong social approval of certain kinds of competence. It is arguable that in some ways we do *not* encourage competence – that we keep our children too dependent for too long, denying them the opportunity to exercise their very considerable capacity for initiative and responsible action. This is perhaps hard to avoid in a complex urban society with a highly developed technology. Yet within the educational system at least there is certainly strong social approval of competence in the more disembedded skills of the mind. So the child who succeeds in coping with these new challenges when he enters school will be highly valued by his teachers – and all too often the one who initially fails will not. In either case the child will quickly discover how he is judged to be doing. That he has often made up his mind about his cognitive competence even before he comes to school is emphasized by Marion Blank, who reports the occurrence of remarks like 'I'm dumb', 'I can't', 'I'm stupid' and 'I don't know how to do things' from certain kindergarten children faced by some cognitive demand.

There can be no doubt that if we decide we cannot cope with a particular kind of challenge we tend to give up and avoid it. Bruner draws a sharp distinction between 'coping' and 'defending' which he likens to the distinction between 'playing tennis on the one hand and fighting like fury to stay off the tennis court altogether on the other'. People do of course differ in the extent to which they persevere in the teeth of persistent failure. Robert the Bruce is said to have observed the tenacity of a spider and resolved to try again. But a spider has presumably no self-image to disturb it, and Robert the Bruce was a mature man who doubtless had a strong and resilient one.

Szasz has this to say on the subject:

> Definers (that is, persons who insist on defining others) are like pathogenic micro-organisms: each invades, parasitizes, and often destroys his victim; and, in each case, those whose resistance is low are the most susceptible to attack. Hence, those whose immunological defences are weak are most likely to contract infectious diseases; and those whose social defences are weak – that is, the young and the old, the sick and the poor, and so forth – are most likely to contract invidious definitions of themselves.

If the child is defined as a failure he will almost certainly fail, at any rate in the things which the definers value; and perhaps later he will hit out very hard against those who so defined him.

So we know at least something to avoid. But we must contrive to avoid it not merely at the surface of our behaviour. If we do not genuinely respect and value the children, I am afraid they will come to know.

Yet important as it is to avoid infecting the children with 'invidious definitions', it is not enough. More than this is called for. When it comes to self-esteem, not even a young child depends entirely for his judgements on the views of others. For he can often see quite well for himself how he is doing. Paquita McMichael, in an interesting study of the relation between early reading skills and the self-image, concluded that there was a good deal of objective truth in the children's assessments of their competence. 'When they agreed that they were not able to do things as well as some other children they were admitting to a reality.'

Thus a very important part of the job of a teacher – or of a parent in a teaching role – is to guide the child towards tasks where he will be able objectively to do well, but not too easily, not without putting forth some effort, not without difficulties to be mastered, errors to be overcome, creative solutions to be found. This means assessing his skills with sensitivity and accuracy, understanding the levels of his confidence and energy, and responding to his errors in helpful ways.

Most teachers would accept this, I daresay, but it is not at all easy to achieve in practice and there is no general formula for success. However, a valuable discussion of teaching episodes where just this kind of thing is being attempted is given in Marion Blank's book: *Teaching Learning in the Pre-school*. She argues that it is essential to permit errors to occur but that the effectiveness of any teaching critically depends on how the wrong responses are then handled by the teacher. She makes many specific practical suggestions about this but she acknowledges that it is not possible at the moment to give rules for the exact application of her technique – it remains an art. Obviously much depends on the child's personality. Ways that work with a passive withdrawn child will not work with a hyperactive impulsive one. And if the child is functioning very poorly it is necessary to concentrate on helping him over his difficulties without too much delay.

It should be noted that Blank developed her techniques for use in a one-to-one teaching situation. She fully recognizes the difficulties of applying them with a group. It remains true that the kinds of teaching decision with which she is concerned are of pervasive importance and that there must surely be gain from any enhanced awareness of them.

The traditional way of encouraging children to want to learn the things that we want to teach is by giving rewards for success: prizes, privileges, gold stars. Two grave risks attend this practice. The first is obvious to common sense, the second much less so.

The obvious risk is to the children who do not get the stars, for this is just one way of defining them as failures. The other risk is to all of the children – 'winners' and 'losers' alike. There is now a substantial amount of evidence pointing to the conclusion that if an activity is rewarded by some extrinsic prize or token – something quite external to the activity itself – then that activity is less likely to be engaged in later in a free and voluntary manner when the rewards are absent, and it is less likely to be enjoyed.

This has now been demonstrated in numerous experiments with people of ages ranging from three or four years to adulthood.

One study, by M. R. Lepper and his colleagues, was carried out in a nursery school. Some of the children were given materials to draw with and were told that they would get a prize for drawing, which they duly did. Other children were given the same materials but with no prizes or talk of prizes. Some days afterwards all of the children were given the opportunity to use these same materials again in a situation where lots of other toys were also available to them. The question was: would the groups differ in the amount of time which they spent in drawing? One might have expected that those who had been rewarded would return more eagerly to the situation which had been 'reinforced'. But the opposite happened. The children who had been rewarded spent a smaller proportion of their time drawing.

If one takes as criterion not the time freely spent on an activity but the person's own statement of how much it has been enjoyed, the same sort of thing is found: extrinsic material reward tends to decrease enjoyment. Children (and adults) who have been given prizes for doing something tend to say that they like it less well than children who have been given none. And there is even some evidence to suggest that the quality of what is produced may decline.

These findings obviously lead on at once to a further question: if you tell a child he is doing well, are you also rewarding him and hence perhaps running the same sort of risk as if you give him a prize? For, after all, verbal approval is a kind of prize. And certainly, like a material object, it is extrinsic to the activity itself – something added on at the end.

The available evidence suggests that the effects of telling someone he has done well are not the same as those of giving him a prize. For instance, R. Anderson, S. T. Manoogian and J. S. Reznick carried out a study very similar to the one by Lepper and his colleagues (see above) except that there were two extra conditions, in one of which the children were praised for their drawings. The results from Lepper's study were confirmed: the giving of material rewards was related to a decrease in time spent on the activity later. But the giving of verbal encouragement had the opposite effect. And this is just as well. If it were not so, teachers would have to face a disconcerting dilemma. For children must know how they are doing. As we have seen, they often have a shrewd idea of this themselves—and some tasks make it very evident. The young children who were given the task of balancing blocks on a narrow bar (see page 107) could see for themselves whether the blocks stayed in place or fell off. So they could develop theories, discover the inadequacies of these theories and develop better theories, all without external reward of any kind. This is part of the justification for 'discovery learning'. But it is not equally possible in all kinds of learning to contrive situations where the child will see for himself the outcome of his efforts. Frequently he must be told. He must be told: 'Good, you've got that right!' or: 'No, that's wrong.* Try again.'

Such comments do more, of course, than merely give objective knowledge of results. They are unquestionably not neutral. But perhaps it is relevant to an understanding of the difference between words of praise and gold stars to draw a distinction between reward and recognition and to acknowledge how strong a need we have to communicate achievement to our fellow men and see it confirmed in their eyes. Thus Gerard Manley Hopkins, who considered that his vocation as a Jesuit was incompatible with the publication of his poetry in his lifetime, reveals in his letters – especially his letters to Robert Bridges – how hard this was for him: 'There is a point with me in matters of any size when I must absolutely have encouragement as much as crops rain . . .' He goes on bravely, '. . . afterwards I am independent.' But many of us do not reach this kind of independence ever. And young children are certainly unlikely to have done so.

The final condition which Anderson and her colleagues included in their study (see page 116) is relevant here. In this condition the experimenter began by declaring an interest in

---

* Notice that, if the child is told 'That's good' whether he has really done well or not, the informational value of the comment is destroyed. It is a subtle art to give genuine information and to encourage at the same time.

'how boys and girls draw pictures' – and thereafter firmly refused to manifest this interest in any way. A child might show a picture, trying, as the report of the study puts it, 'to elicit some recognition or validation'. But he got none. The experimenter ignored all such overtures, turning his face away and saying: 'I've got work to do.' It is not surprising to learn that the children who received this treatment showed the greatest drop of all in the time which they later spent in drawing.

This still leaves us with the question of why extrinsic material rewards tend to produce effects of damaging kinds. The explanation which fits the known facts most nearly would seem to be that we enjoy best and engage most readily in activities which we *experience as freely chosen*. We do not like being controlled, we like controlling ourselves. Insofar as reward is seen as a means of controlling our behaviour, it tends to diminish our interest and our pleasure. Of course we may work hard to get the reward at the time and for so long as we expect more reward to be forthcoming but we will be less likely to go on with the activity when the reward is withdrawn.

This is strikingly illustrated by the following story (quoted by E. L. Deci in his book *Intrinsic Motivation*).

In a little Southern town where the Klan was riding again, a Jewish tailor had the temerity to open his little shop on the main street. To drive him out of the town the Kleagle of the Klan set a gang of little ragamuffins to annoy him. Day after day they stood at the entrance of his shop. 'Jew! Jew!' they hooted at him. The situation looked serious for the tailor. He took the matter so much to heart that he began to brood and spent sleepless nights over it. Finally out of desperation he evolved a plan.

The following day, when the little hoodlums came to jeer at him, he came to the door and said to them, 'From today on any boy who calls me "Jew" will get a dime from me.' Then he put his hand in his pocket and gave each boy a dime.

Delighted with their booty, the boys came back the following day and began to shrill, 'Jew! Jew!' The tailor came out smiling. He put his hand in his pocket and gave each of the boys a nickel, saying, 'A dime is too much – I can only afford a nickel today.' The boys went away satisfied because, after all, a nickel was money, too.

However, when they returned the next day to hoot at him, the tailor gave them only a penny each.

'Why do we only get a penny today?' they yelled.

'That's all I can afford.'

'But two days ago you gave us a dime, and yesterday we got a nickel. It's not fair, mister.'

'Take it or leave it. That's all you're going to get!'

'Do you think we're going to call you "Jew" for one lousy penny?'

'So don't!'

And they didn't.

All of this leads to a central dilemma for those who want to teach the young. There is a compelling case for control. The young child is not capable of deciding for himself what he should learn: he is quite simply too ignorant. And he needs our help to sustain him through the actual process of learning. Whitehead puts it vividly: 'After all the child is the heir to long ages of civilization and it is absurd to let him wander in the intellectual maze of men in the Glacial Epoch.'

On the other hand, we should never forget the children who, having learned to shout 'Jew' for a dime, would not then shout it when the payment came to an end. And there is clear evidence that if we try to exercise the control not by reward but by punishment the negative effects are even greater. If, when they leave us, our pupils turn away from what we have taught them, the teaching has surely been in vain.

Those who are most keenly aware of this latter danger tend to call themselves 'progressive' and to advocate 'freedom'. Those who are most keenly aware of the former danger – the danger of leaving children to wander in the intellectual mazes of pre-history – are the advocates of 'formal education' and of 'discipline'.

I can see only one way out of this dilemma: it is to exercise such control as is needful with a light touch and never to relish the need. It is possible after all for control to be more or less obtrusive, more or less paraded. Also a great deal will depend on what the teacher sees the aim of the control to be. If the ultimate aim of the control is to render itself unnecessary, if the teacher obviously wants the children to become competent, self-determining, responsible beings and believes them capable of it, then I am convinced that the risk of rejection of learning will be much diminished. We come back thus to the question of whether the teacher truly respects the children and lets them see it. If this condition is met, then the guidance of learning within a structured environment will not be seen as the action of a warder behind prison bars.

11. The Shape of Minds to Come

To conclude, then, here is the heart of the matter. By the time they come to school, all normal children can show skill as thinkers and language-users to a degree which must compel our respect, so long as they are dealing with 'real-life' meaningful situations in which they have purposes and intentions and in which they can recognize and respond to similar purposes and intentions in others. (Sometimes, as in the story context, it is enough that they recognize them in others.) These human intentions are the matrix in which the child's thinking is embedded. They sustain and direct his thoughts and his speech, just as they sustain and direct the thought and the speech of adults – even intellectually sophisticated adults – most of the time.

While the child's thinking and his language remain wholly within the bounds of human sense in this kind of way, he remains largely unaware of them. He is conscious of the outer world that he is dealing with and of his goals in that world. Thus he cannot fail to be aware of himself as an agent in that world, coping with it. But he has only a very limited awareness of the means that he uses for coping and he does not reflect upon them in abstraction from the contexts in which he employs them. He uses his skills to serve his compelling immediate purposes. But he does not notice how he uses them, and so he cannot call them into service deliberately when the compelling purpose has gone.

Education, as it has developed in our kind of culture, requires him to be able to do just that – to call the powers of his mind into service *at will* and use them to tackle problems which do not arise out of the old familiar matrix but which are 'posed' – presented in abrupt isolation and presented, to begin with at least, by some other person whose purposes are obscure.

A sense that such demands are 'unnatural' – as indeed in a sense they are – has led many concerned educators to argue that demands of any kind should be minimal – that the children should rather be offered *opportunities* to learn, that they should be encouraged to ask their own questions and be helped to solve these when they genuinely want to know the answer, that they should express themselves spontaneously and be unconstrained.

Behind arguments of this last kind there is often, explicitly or implicitly, some metaphor of the kind that Froebel used, some image of the child as a growing plant that risks being stunted in the darkness and in the cold dry soil of the traditional class-room or trained to some twisted and perverse shape by the teacher's harsh pruning-shears.

The risks are real enough. But human children are not plants with only one 'natural' way of growing. They are beings of richly varied possibilities, and they are beings with potential for guiding their own growth in the end. They can learn to be conscious of the powers of their own minds and decide to what ends they will use them. However, they cannot do this without help – or at least it would be a long slow business and few would make much headway.

Carl Jung was not overly fond of people whom he described as 'intellectuals'. He says of one patient, who had behaved in a way of which he strongly disapproved: 'But this patient was not really a criminal, only a so-called intellectual who believed so much in the power of reason that he even thought he could unthink a wrong he had committed.' Yet this realization of the dangers of an unbalanced development of the intellect did not blind Jung to what he calls its 'power and dignity'. Also he was very clear about the importance of school and about its main function: 'School', he tells us, 'is in fact a means of strengthening in a purposeful way the integration of consciousness.' And the development of consciousness is 'what they [the children] need more than anything else' at this stage in their lives. In this, somewhat unexpectedly, Jung comes close to Vygotsky who, as we have seen, regards 'consciousness and deliberate mastery' as 'the principal contributions of the school years'.

The point to grasp is how closely the growth of consciousness is related to the growth of the intellect. The two are not synonymous, for the growth of consciousness has much wider implications – but the link with intellectual growth is none the less intimate and profound. If the intellectual powers are to develop, the child must gain a measure of control over his own thinking and he cannot control it while he remains unaware of it. The attaining of this control means prising thought out of its primitive unconscious embeddedness in the immediacies of living in the world and interacting with other human beings. It means learning to move beyond the bounds of human sense. It is on this movement that all the higher intellectual skills depend.

The process of moving beyond the bounds of human sense is unnatural in the sense that it does not happen spontaneously. The very possibility of this movement is the product of long ages of culture; and the possibility is not realized in the life of an individual child unless the resources of the culture are marshalled in a sustained effort directed to that end.

But in another sense the movement is not unnatural at all – it is merely the fostering of latent power. And it certainly need not involve harsh or repressive discipline or blind drilling or deadening instruction of the kind that has led so many sensitive people in the past to reject 'formal schooling' and that led William Blake to write:

> But to go to school on a summer morn
> O! it drives all joy away!
> Under a cruel eye outworn
> The little ones spend the day
> In sighing and dismay.

Indeed, it *must not* involve these things, or the purpose will be defeated.

This was the conclusion reached at the end of the previous chapter; while the point from which the first chapter began was precisely that schooling at present turns into a wretched experience for many children, however happily it may begin, and that something most urgently needs to be done to change this.

The experience becomes wretched at present largely because it is a wretched thing to be compelled to do something at which you persistently fail. The older children are frequently not meeting the demands of school successfully and they know they are being written off as stupid, however vigorously they may defend themselves against the knowledge. 'We get interested in what we get good at', to quote Bruner's simple statement of a central truth. Thus many of our children grow bored and disheartened.

One course that seems to offer a way out, as we have seen, is for schools not to make the demands which cause the trouble. If this is done, then for a time the children may play happily enough – and accordingly the discontent often does not manifest itself until the later years at school, when the demands of society at large for literacy, numeracy, scientific understanding and so on can no longer be pushed aside or denied.

Since these demands spring from deep-rooted considerations of social value, they would not be easy to change. The practical usefulness of the intellectual skills is not the only thing involved in the value judgements, but it would be enough by itself. Whether we like it or not, we need these skills – and, collectively, we know it.

The issue, then, is whether we must accept it as inevitable that only a small minority of people can ever develop intellectually to a high level of competence. I believe that we do not have to accept this. I believe that the *nature* of the very considerable difficulty which these skills present to the human mind has not been adequately recognized. Although we have known for a long time that 'abstract thinking' is hard, we have lacked a sufficiently clear – and widespread – understanding of what is involved in moving beyond the bounds of human sense and learning to manipulate our own thinking in the new disembedded modes, free from the old involvements, which sustain and hamper at the same time. I also believe that, once we do recognize these things, we shall be able to help many children to become competent thinkers in these new modes, if we choose to do so; and I have tried to make some practical suggestions to this end. Of course, about the question of *how* this can be done there is much to discover. It is a great mistake to suppose that, once knowledge has been gained, the application of that knowledge to serve practical ends comes automatically. However, I see no reason to doubt that, with the right sort of directed effort and with enough social commitment to the enterprise, our knowledge *could* be applied in such a way as to make a substantial difference.

And what then? Would we find ourselves back at the Gates of Eden? Or rather (since clearly that is not quite appropriate!) would we stand at the doors of a new Eden – a sort of paradise for intellectuals?

That is the stuff of which a certain kind of science fiction is made and it is calculated to produce a shudder along the spines of most of us – not without reason.

It is the kind of image which C. S. Lewis holds up for us to hate when one of his villains is 'urging the promotion of "objectivity" ':

> 'Before going on', said Frost, 'I must ask you to be strictly objective. Resentment and fear are both chemical phenomena. Our reactions to one another are chemical phenomena. Social relations are chemical relations . . . A circle bound together by subjective feelings of mutual confidence and liking would be useless. They could all, in principle, be produced by injections.'

And later (Frost speaking again):

> 'In the new age, what has hitherto been merely the intellectual nucleus of the race is to become, by gradual stages, the race itself . . . The individual is to become all head. The human race is to become all Technocracy.'

It is certainly no accident that Lewis's character is given the name 'Frost'. There is good cause to call the intellect 'cold' – it is cold by definition because it must operate in detachment from human sense and all the warm-blooded links which that mode of functioning has with emotion. 'Disembedded' is not too far from 'disembodied'. But of course this does not mean that an individual must become cold as a result of developing intellectual competence. Only a quite one-sided development which, as Jung puts it, causes one to 'violate the feeling-values' has this kind of effect. And, somewhat paradoxically, if we got better at helping people to develop intellectually there might be less danger of this very one-sidedness. For there has been a long tyranny of the intellect and it is this which has led to the risk of distortion, personal and social.

I suspect that we can attribute the firm grip of this tyranny to two influences working together: first, the extreme practical usefulness of the intellectual skills (demonstrated to varying degrees from the days when writing was first used to keep records until the days when British mathematicians broke the German 'Enigma' cipher in the Second World War); and second, their rarity. They will not become less useful; but what would happen if they were to become less rare?

It would be wise not to underestimate the social changes that might then follow. For we are not talking only about getting more people to spell correctly or learn their multiplication tables – the sorts of modest, safe achievement for which there is currently such great demand. These things would be achieved no doubt – but these would be the least of the changes.

The existence within society of a powerful, intellectual élite, with a strong sense of superiority, is by no means a recent thing. We have seen in Chapter 7 that this state of affairs already obtained as long ago as 2000 BC in the Egypt of the Middle Kingdom when, as now, literacy and its attendant skills were seen as ways of raising status; when, as now, there was concomitant denigration of the human hand.

What has changed since then is merely the cut-off point – or set of cut-off points – and the fact that our metal-workers and laundrymen, having all attended the Writing Schools, have perhaps a more acute sense of personal failure and dissatisfaction than their Ancient Egyptian counterparts. Radical change would mean that the majority of our children would leave our Writing Schools with a strong sense of having succeeded there. Evidently they could not all be 'top of the class'. But, if we could contrive to lessen a little our preoccupation with rank order, they might leave with feelings of competence and self-respect.

And after they left, what would then become of them? What would they do with their lives? How would they use their skills?

These questions reveal already that, if most of our citizens became competent in the exercise of intellectual skills, we would have to come to a higher valuing of at least some other skills and functions – the ones obviously necessary to the conduct of our lives – for we could no longer regard these activities as the province of the educational failures.

Perhaps it is the convenience of having educational failures which explains why we have tolerated so many of them for so long and which accounts for what Whitehead calls 'the frivolous inertia' with which the whole question of education is still treated today.

A vigorous self-confident young population of educational successes would not be easy to employ on our present production lines. So we might at last be forced to face up to the problem of making it more attractive to work in our factories – and elsewhere – and, if we had done our job in the schools really well, we should expect to find that economic attractions would not be enough. We might be compelled at last to look seriously for ways of making working lives more satisfying.

It is fortunate that the human love of working with the hand is hard to suppress. Perhaps we can even attribute the denigration of work with the hand to this fact. Perhaps long ago, when literate civilization began, it seemed as if the only way to get people to value the intellect and work at its development was to make them scorn the skills of the body.

In the life of a child, joy in the immediate involvement of the body in skilled activity comes early and spontaneously. As we have seen already, this is by no means an unthinking joy, but it is not reflective. The later exercise of the reflective capacities can bring joy too – but this is a joy that does not come unaided. The more expert we become at giving the help that is necessary to evoke it, the less will be the need to use the technique of *The Satire on the Trades* as a means of keeping reluctant noses to an academic grind-stone.

Thus if at last we become really good at helping large

numbers of people to the experience of intellectual satisfaction, we should have more freedom to turn to the development of human potentials of other kinds. Certainly it should
not then be too hard – or too dangerous – to reinstate the
human hand. And the probable result would be a vast release
of creative energy.

Beyond this, I leave speculation to the futurologists. But if we
are not willing to try and to keep trying, in the light of
knowledge attained, to help our children meet the demands
which we impose on them, then we must not call them stupid.
We must rather call ourselves indifferent or afraid.

Appendix: Piaget's Theory of Intellectual Development

Contents

The main text of this book has contained some discussion of the work of Jean Piaget, and I have tried to make this discussion intelligible even to a reader with no background knowledge. However, there has been no way to avoid leaving such a reader with a quite inadequate impression of Piaget's theoretical claims. For the theory is a massive construction, and only limited parts of it have been relevant to what I have had to say. This appendix is an attempt to correct the imbalance and provide a better – though still necessarily incomplete – picture of the whole. I shall not try here to present the evidence with which Piaget supports his claims, except occasionally by way of illustration; and I shall not be concerned with critical evaluation. The aim is to give a brief and clear account of the main features of the theory.

1.   The General Nature of the Theory

Piaget was originally trained as a zoologist, and when he studies human behaviour he tries to place it in the wider context of the behaviour of other living things. For him the key question is: how do animals adapt to their environment? Human intelligence is then considered as one means of doing this.

It is important to recognize that the focus of attention is not on the ways in which people differ from one another – hence not on 'intelligence testing' as ordinarily understood. Piaget wants to discover – and explain – the normal course of development. For he believes that there *is* a normal course: a sequence which we all follow, though we go at varying speeds and some go further than others.

This focus on what is common to us all is related to the fact that, as well as being a zoologist, Piaget is an epistemologist: that is, he is concerned with general questions about the nature of knowledge. He believes that these questions cannot be answered without taking account of how knowledge develops and grows. So both of his interests – the biological and the epistemological – converge in the study of human intellectual development.

Clearly this development can be studied as it occurs in individual lives; or it can be studied as it occurs in the history of the species – in the development of bodies of knowledge like mathematics or the sciences. Piaget is interested in both of these topics. But we shall be concerned here only with his claims about the developments that take place within an individual life span.

In order to understand these claims, it is best to begin by considering what he has to say about biological adaptation in general.

2. Features of Biological Adaptation

2.1 *Self-regulation and Equilibrium.* In Piaget's view, the essential thing about living organisms is that they are *self-regulating systems.* Unlike non-living things, they can maintain or repair their own structures in case of threat or damage. To take two familiar physiological examples, we have ways of restoring damaged tissue if we cut a finger, and we have ways of keeping body temperature steady within narrow limits even when the temperature around us varies widely.

Thus living things try to achieve a kind of stability of organization in the face of danger. When they quite fail to do this, they die. Since they all die in the end, perfect adaptation is never attained: some new threat may always come along and prove defeating. However, it is clear that the wider the range of events that an animal can cope with, the better its chances. Some animals are very well adapted to a particular limited environment but are not flexible. They cannot change their behaviour when the environment changes. Human beings, however, have an outstanding capacity for flexible responsive change.

When an animal has achieved a kind of harmony – or satisfactory pattern of interaction – with its environment, Piaget would say that it is in *equilibrium.* This equilibrium, however, is not to be thought of as a state of rest. It is a state of continual activity, in which the organism compensates for – or cancels out – disturbances to the system, either actual or anticipated. That is, the compensation may be a correction for something that has already gone wrong; or it may be a preparation for something that is expected to go wrong if nothing is done.

2.2 *Assimilation and Accommodation.* This emphasis on activity is to be found throughout Piaget's thinking. A living creature does not merely react, it also *takes action.* Adaptation is not just a matter of changing when there is pressure to change, in the sort of passive way in which, for instance, a lump of dough will change shape when squeezed. The difference is that the living being has an organization to preserve. So one aspect of biological adaptation is the effort to deal with the environment by making it fit into the organism's own existing structures – by 'incorporating' it, in some sense of that term. Literal 'incorporation' takes place, for instance, when an animal digests food. The general name which Piaget gives to this part of the adaptive process is *assimilation*.

It is clear, however, that the drive to assimilate could not be effective if it functioned alone. If an animal is going to adapt successfully, it must modify its behaviour in ways that recognize the properties of the things it is dealing with. It can drink liquids, for instance, but it has to chew solid foods if they are to be assimilated at all. So assimilation never occurs in pure form but is always balanced by at least some component of *accommodation*. Accommodation is the effort to fit the behaviour of the organism to the environment; thus the two processes are opposed, but complementary.

While assimilation and accommodation can be thought of separately, they cannot really be distinguished from one another in any adaptive act. It is not possible to observe behaviour and say: 'Aha, now the animal is assimilating and now it is accommodating.' Both processes are going on together, indissolubly linked. It is through their joint action that the animal can achieve both continuity and novelty. Assimilation works for preservation of structures; accommodation works for variability, growth and change.

Adaptive behaviour always contains some of each of these two components. They may occur, however, in varying proportions. Piaget often quotes the make-believe play of a young child as an example of behaviour rich in assimilative tendencies. For in the course of this play the child is not greatly concerned about the objective characteristics of the things he plays with. An old bit of wood can serve as a doll or a ship or an aeroplane, according to the needs and interests of the moment. By contrast, imitation provides an example of behaviour that is mainly (never purely) accommodatory, for it is an attempt to act in a way shaped by features of the external world.

Though extremes of this kind occur, adaptation will be at its most effective when there is due balance between the two tendencies. To describe this balance Piaget makes further use of the word 'equilibrium'. And while he recognizes that some kinds of equilibrium between assimilation and accommodation can occur at all levels of development, he argues that, as a child grows up, more satisfactory forms of balance between the two are achieved. (This achievement is held to be related to increases in the ability to 'decentre' – see section 4.5.)

3. Human Intelligence: the Course of Development

3.1 *The Conquest of an Extended Environment.* All adaptation tends towards the development of ability to deal with a wider environment. But human intelligence is unique in the extent to which this is achieved. Most animals adapt only to things close to them in space and time; and this is true of human infants also. But as children develop, they become able to acquire knowledge of, and to think about, objects and events quite remote from them. One of Piaget's main concerns is to show how this change comes about.

3.2 *Continuity and Change.* Although Piaget insists that development is continuous, he does allow for the existence of stages. During any given stage many superficially different patterns of behaviour can of course be seen to occur. Underlying them, however, there is held to be some common structure which explains them and gives the stage its unity. So transition to a new stage means that some fairly fundamental re-organization is taking place. There is, however, no sharp break between stages and there are no completely new beginnings.

3.3 *Order and Speed.* The main stages follow one another in an order that is held to be the same for all children. But this is not because they are 'pre-programmed' or wholly determined by maturation (see section 4.2). It is because each stage builds on the one before it. Thus the earlier construction is necessary for the later one. While the order of the stages is the same for all children, however, the speed of movement certainly is not. The ages quoted by Piaget are intended as averages. The

133

existence of wide departures from them is recognized. There are held to be three main stages, or periods, with certain sub-divisions.

3.4 *The Sensori-motor Period (birth to 18 months, approximately).* At birth the child has a very limited range of things he can do; and at first sight his equipment seems poor. He can make only a small number of reflex responses – sucking, swallowing and the like. However, the reflexes are not to be thought of as isolated responses, for they are embedded in a wider pattern of spontaneous rhythmic activity; and the infant already has the capacity to set in motion the complex processes of assimilation and accommodation which will transform the rigid reflexes into surprisingly flexible patterns of behaviour before the first period is over.

During this time, the reflexes develop through a series of sub-stages (Piaget recognizes six of them) into organized behaviour patterns (or schemas) which can be used intentionally. The child becomes capable of inventing new means of doing things. Thus he can solve certain problems on a practical level. For instance, he can devise ways of getting things which are out of his reach by using simple tools.

These changes can be seen readily enough in behaviour. But at the same time Piaget argues that a most important transformation is going on which cannot be observed in this direct way. The claim is that to begin with the child is unable to make any distinction between himself and the rest of the world. He does not know initially that anything else exists; and by the same token he does not really know that he exists either. He is profoundly egocentric.

To understand what Piaget means by this it is essential to grasp the fact that the egocentrism he is talking about at this stage is totally unconscious. There can be no self-awareness in it. So it is very far removed from any such notions as 'pre-occupation with the self' or 'selfishness'.

In the course of the sensori-motor period, the child slowly manages to reduce this deep primitive unawareness. He begins to distinguish himself from the rest of the world. By the end of the period, he has constructed the notion of a world of objects which are independent of him and of his actions. He knows that things go on existing when he cannot see them or sense them in any way.

Evidence that this fundamental change takes place during the sensori-motor period is held to be provided by the child's behaviour when an object with which he is playing is hidden from him – say by a cloth placed over it. Up to the age of six months or so, he makes no attempt to recover the object. This is taken to mean that he still has no *object concept* – no idea of the independent existence of other things. The argument then is that his gradual progress in constructing such a concept is reflected in his increasing skill at working out where an object has gone, first in the simple case already described, later in more complex cases where the object is moved from one place to another.

Thus the development of the object concept is considered to be closely bound up with the progressive organizing of movements in space – both the movements of objects and the movements of the child himself from one place to another. When the development is complete the child can follow an object through a succession of movements even if it is not visible to him all the time; and he can find his own way around, making detours and returning to the place from which he started. Piaget claims that these abilities depend upon the formation of a fundamental structure called 'the group of displacements'.

The term 'group' is defined and illustrated in the next section (3.5). Meanwhile it may be said that the most important feature of group organization, so far as Piaget's theory is concerned, is *reversibility*. Once the group of displacements is established the child can reverse a movement from A to B, so as to get back to A again. The full significance of this will become more clear when the developments of the concrete operational period are discussed.

3.5 *The Concrete Operational Period* (*18 months to 11 years approximately*). This long stage is divided into two sub-periods. During the first of these, which is called the 'preoperational period' and which lasts until around the age of seven, the 'concrete operations' are being prepared for; during the second they are being established and consolidated.

Evidence that the operations are functioning is provided, according to the theory, by the child's response to such tasks as conservation (see page 61) and class inclusion (see page 42). When a child reasons, for instance, that the number of a set of objects must remain the same although its arrangement in space has been altered, he is said to do this by understanding that the original arrangement could be reached again merely by reversing the movements that changed it. Thus his thought is reversible.

This kind of mental flexibility is closely related to a postulated increase in the ability to 'decentre' (section 4.5) and is held to depend on the development of operational structures. But what *are* these structures?

In Piaget's theory the word 'operation' has a precise meaning. To understand it, three things must be grasped.

First, operations are actions. It is true that they are not physical manipulations, for they are carried out 'in the mind' only. But they are actions nonetheless; and they have their origin in the physical acts of the sensori-motor period.

Second, the acts in which they originate are not just any acts whatever. Rather they are such acts as combining, ordering, separating and recombining things. Thus they are acts of great generality.

Third, an operation cannot exist on its own, but only within an organized system of operations. And the organization always has the form of a 'group' or a 'grouping'.

The nature of group organization will be easy to understand if we take a familiar example. In any group there has to be a set of elements: let us take as our example the set of positive and negative whole numbers. Also there has to be an operation that can be carried out on the elements: let us consider the operation of addition. The following four conditions must then be satisfied.

(1) COMPOSITION
If the operation is carried out on any two elements, the result is also an element – that is, one never gets outside of the system. (If you add one number to another number you get a third number.)

(2) ASSOCIATIVITY
The order in which two successive operations is carried out does not matter. (If you add *three* to *four* and then add *two* you get the same result as you would get by adding *four* to *two* and then adding *three*.)

(3) IDENTITY
Among the elements there is always one, and only one,

identity element. The identity element does not alter any other element with which it is combined. (The identity element where numbers are being added is *zero*. If you add *zero* to a given number, the result is simply that number.)

(4) REVERSIBILITY
Every element has another element called its inverse. When an element is combined with its inverse the result is the identity element. (Positive and negative numbers are the inverse of one another. *Three* added to *minus three* gives *zero*.)

A group is a mathematical structure. But Piaget believes that it is of great psychological importance because it can be used to specify the nature of some of the fundamental structures of human intelligence, ranging from the first organization of that intelligence on a practical level (section 3.4) to its final organization on a highly abstract symbolic plane (section 3.6). In between, however, at the concrete operational stage, it turns out that the group structure will not quite 'fit' or correspond to the structures of the mind. For instance, it does not correspond perfectly to the structure of a hierarchy of classes and sub-classes; for if one thinks of trying to add a class to itself one finds that this does not yield a new class, as would be the case with numbers. (Three plus three equals six, but the class of dogs added to the class of dogs merely equals the class of dogs.)

Because of this kind of difficulty, Piaget introduces the notion of a 'grouping'. A grouping is a kind of variant of a group, specially adapted to take account of the structures of classification, seriation and the like. (For details the reader is referred to Piaget's own account in *Logic and Psychology*.) The important thing to note is that, in spite of the differences between 'group' and 'grouping', the reversibility condition in some form is always maintained; and for Piaget's theory this is the essential feature. Thus if two sub-classes are added to form a total class, it is always possible to take one of them away again. And when thought has become operational if is possible to do this 'in the mind'.

The preparatory work that has to take place during the pre-operational period before the operations come into being consists mainly in the development of the child's capacity to represent things to himself. As we have seen, the group structure exists already by the end of the sensori-motor period (section 3.4), but on a practical level only. The next step is to 'internalize' it. But Piaget insists again and again that internalizing a structure is not just a matter of somehow taking it in whole – any more than knowledge in general is a matter of receiving a ready-made 'copy' of reality. Internalizing means rebuilding on a new plane. The work of the sensori-motor period has to be done all over again. But now the building-blocks are symbols in the mind: acts of thought rather than acts of the body. A child of two or three can put objects in a row, space them out, and put them together again. A child of seven or eight can *think* of doing these things.

However, the new symbolic acts are still closely tied to the concrete things on which the original physical acts were performed. The child is still mainly thinking about doing things with physical objects: ordering them, classifying them, arranging them in series and so on. Hence the name *concrete* operational period.

When Piaget compares sensori-motor intelligence with the intelligence of the concrete operational period he speaks of three main ways in which the latter represents an advance on the former.

First, sensori-motor intelligence is more static, less mobile. It considers things one after another, without managing an overview. It is like a film run slowly, almost a succession of stills. Operational intelligence is much better at dealing with transformations between states and seeing how they relate to one another.

Second, sensori-motor intelligence aims only at practical success. The operational thinker has much more interest in explanation and understanding. This change is related to developments in consciousness which bring increased awareness of how goals are achieved.

Third, since sensori-motor intelligence is limited to real actions performed on real objects it has a narrow range in space and time. Symbolic actions can roam more widely.

In principle, of course, the range of such acts is unlimited, reaching infinity and eternity. In practice, the range continues to be considerably more restricted so long as thought is still in the concrete period.

3.6 *The Formal Operational Period.* The thinking of this period, once it has been consolidated, is the thinking of the intelligent adult. Its most marked feature is the ability to reason logically, starting from premises and drawing the conclusions which necessarily follow. And it does not now matter, according to the theory, whether or not the premises are true: they can be accepted as mere postulates.

This ability to work from postulates, or hypotheses, underlies not only logical and mathematical thought, but also the kind of activity that is characteristic of science. The formal operational thinker can entertain hypotheses, deduce consequences and use these deductions to put the hypotheses to the test. Further, he can do this by planning systematic experiments in which he will realize, for instance, the value of holding one thing constant while letting other things vary. And he can then go on to formulate general rules based on the experimental findings.

Piaget tries various ways of capturing the essence of the change from the concrete to the formal period. For instance, he says that, while the concrete operational thinker is still concerned to manipulate *things* even if he does this 'in the mind', the formal operational thinker has become able to manipulate *propositions*, or ideas. He can reason on the basis of verbal statements. Piaget quotes as an example the following problem:

Edith is fairer than Susan. Edith is darker than Lily. Who is the darkest?

This problem gives considerable difficulty to many children of ten. Yet if it were a question of arranging three dolls in serial order, the task would be easy for them.

Piaget uses this kind of difference to support the claim that, once again, the development of the formal period is a matter of reconstructing on a new plane what was achieved at the preceding level.

In this case, the process of reconstruction leads to a further important outcome, which is perhaps best expressed as a shift in the relation between what is real and what is possible. The formal operational thinker tends to start from the possible. This means that, when he tackles a problem, he is likely to begin by considering possibilities in a systematic way. So then 'the facts' are placed in a wider context. They come to be thought of as a kind of realized part of a wider universe consisting of what might be.

Perhaps the best illustration of the effect of this shift is given by a task which consists in trying to discover ways of combining colourless chemicals so as to produce a yellow liquid. The formal operational thinker is the one who systematically tries all the possible combinations. Typically, unlike the child of the concrete period, he does not stop when he has found one method that works. He goes on until he has explored the whole system.

Finally, Piaget once more uses the concept of the group when he describes the structures underlying formal operational thought. And now he proposes that the various elementary 'groupings' of the concrete operational period are replaced by one unified group called the 'Four-group' or the INRC group. It is unfortunately impossible to give an adequate description of this group without entering into considerable complexities. Readers who want to know more should consult Piaget's own account in *Logic and Psychology*.

4. Human Intelligence: Theoretical Notions

4.1 *The Role of Action*. Piaget asserts that there is no discontinuity between the simplest kinds of adaptive behaviour and the most highly evolved forms of intelligence. The one grows out of the other. Thus even when intelligence has developed to the point where it makes much use of highly abstract knowledge, we must look for the origins of that knowledge in *action*.

Piaget tells us again and again that knowledge does not come to us from outside, 'ready-made'. It is not a 'copy' of reality – not just a matter of receiving impressions, as if our minds were photographic plates. Nor is knowledge something we are born with. We must *construct* it. We do this slowly, over many years.

4.2 *The Role of Maturation*. Piaget's theory is therefore not a maturationist one. We do not become capable of intelligent thought merely by waiting for time to pass. It is true that he allows some role to the maturing of the nervous system. But this does no more than 'open possibilities' or temporarily limit them. The possibilities have to be turned into realities by other means.

4.3 *The Role of the Symbolic Function in General and of Language in Particular.* Piaget insists that language does not create intelligent thought.

He sees language as only one manifestation of what he calls the 'general symbolic function'. When this function first begins to appear, which normally happens during the second year of life, the child becomes able to represent absent objects or events by means of symbols or signs. Piaget distinguishes symbols, which resemble the things they represent, from signs, which stand for things in a quite arbitrary way. Symbols can be private and personal, whereas signs are conventional and 'collective'. Thus language is a system of signs.

The advent of the general symbolic function shows itself, then, not only in the beginnings of language but also in the appearance of make-believe play and in 'deferred imitation' (imitation when the model is no longer present). Piaget believes that internalized imitation is the source of mental imagery.

The general ability to represent reality to oneself is clearly of great importance in the development of thinking. Much of the difference between sensori-motor and operational intelligence, for instance, consists in the fact that the latter is internalized – that is, it functions on a level of representation. And Piaget allows that the more developed intelligence becomes, the greater is the importance of language proper – that is, language as distinct from other manifestations of the symbolic function. But he is never prepared to allow that language is the source of thought. For him, the origins of thought are to be found in action.

4.4 *The Role of the Social Environment.* Piaget accepts that speed of movement through the periods of development is influenced by the social and cultural environment (though the order of the stages remains unaffected). Everything depends, however, on whether the child can assimilate what the environment affords. And this in turn of course, is held to depend on his own constructive efforts. (See also section 4.8 on equilibration and learning.)

At the same time, Piaget recognizes the importance of the exchange of ideas for the development of thought – and in particular for strengthening the awareness of the existence of other points of view.

4.5 *Decentration.** The concepts of 'decentration' and of 'egocentrism' are very closely linked in Piaget's thinking. Decrease in egocentrism amounts to increase in the ability to 'decentre' – that is, to move freely from one point of view to another, either in the literal or the metaphorical sense.

In his earlier writings, Piaget described this process mainly in terms of diminishing egocentrism. Later, he frequently chooses to speak rather of 'centration' and 'decentration'. But this does not indicate any radical change of mind on his part and it certainly does not mean that he is attaching any less importance to the underlying notion. If anything, greater weight is given to it in his later theorizing. The idea of decreasing egocentrism, as he originally used it, was closely associated with that of increasing socialization. More recently he has said: 'But it is far more general and more fundamental to knowledge in all its forms.'

The idea is that when thought is 'centred' by being unable to free itself from one point of view then assimilation has a distorting effect, a satisfactory equilibrium between assimilation and accommodation is not achieved, and only a 'subjective' knowledge of reality can be obtained. The process of improving this knowledge does not then consist in adding more bits of information. It consists rather in developing the ability to move flexibly from one point of view to another – and back again – so as to come closer to an 'objective' view of the whole.

4.6 *Physical Experience, Logico-mathematical Experience and Reflective Abstraction.* Experience, as Piaget uses the term, involves the acquiring of new knowledge through acting on objects. But this process allows different kinds of knowledge to develop. So one may speak, correspondingly, of different kinds of experience. The two kinds which are most important for his theorizing are physical experience and logico-mathematical experience.

Physical experience yields knowledge of the properties of objects that are acted upon. Logico-mathematical experience yields knowledge not of the objects but of the actions themselves and their results.

* For further discussion, see Chapter 2 of the main text of this book.

From physical experience, for instance, one would gain knowledge of the weight of objects; or of the fact that, other things being equal, weight increases as volume increases; and so on.

Now the weight of an object exists even if we do not act at all.* But we may, by our actions, introduce attributes into the world which were not there before. For instance, we may take a number of pebbles and arrange them in a row. We have then introduced an element of order. Suppose that we next count the pebbles and arrive at a certain sum; after which we change the order, count them and arrive at the same sum again. We have thus found out, Piaget claims, that the number of a set of objects is independent of the order in which they are arranged. And this he considers to be a good example of the kind of knowledge that is based on logico-mathematical experience. What we have discovered is a relation between two actions and not, or not only, a property belonging to pebbles.

It is important to notice that the kinds of action which yield logico-mathematical experience are the very same kinds which provide the basis for the operational structures (sections 3.5 and 3.6).

When Piaget speaks of logico-mathematical experience he is making once more the point that even the highest forms of abstract reasoning have their origins in action. The claim is that conclusions which will later be arrived at by deduction – and which indeed will come to seem quite self-evident – must in the beginning be checked against the evidence of what one finds by doing. For example, suppose that a child finds he can arrange a set of objects into two equal sub-divisions, matching them one by one. Will he then *know*, without having to try it, that if one more object is added to the total set, it will no longer be possible to divide the set equally into two in this way? Piaget's answer is that in the pre-operational stage he will not know this, but later it will come to appear utterly obvious to him.

* Notice, however, that since we normally come to *know* an object's weight by picking it up, our knowledge is not independent of action. Thus Piaget argues that physical experience is never 'pure' but always implies at least some logico-mathematical component.

It is in discussing how this kind of change comes about that Piaget introduces the notion of *reflective abstraction*. Processes of abstraction are held to be involved in both physical experience and logico-mathematical experience. In the case of physical experience, knowledge of weight is arrived at by a kind of abstraction which amounts to disregarding other properties of the object such as its volume or its shape. Weight is thus abstracted, or 'taken out' from the whole, in order to be considered. But more than this has to happen when a property is being abstracted from one's own actions. Piaget argues that it is then not enough simply to disregard other properties. In addition, a process of new construction is called for. To use his own words: 'abstraction starting from actions . . . does not consist in merely isolating or noting separated elements, but necessarily requires a reconstruction by means of elements projected or "reflected" from the lower to the higher plane.' It is this kind of reconstruction which is held to take place when, for instance, the concrete operations come into being.

There are two reasons why Piaget describes abstraction starting from actions as 'reflective'. First, as the quotation shows, he is really using a metaphor: the construction on the lower level is 'reflected' or 'projected' up on to the higher level. And second, increased 'reflection', in the sense of enhanced thoughtfulness and consciousness, marks the change.

4.7 *Equilibration.* The importance of *equilibrium* in the theory has already been indicated (section 2.1). *Equilibration* is the general name for the process by which better equilibrium is achieved.

The idea is very closely akin to that of self-regulation (section 2.1). Equilibration is a self-regulatory process and as such it is aimed at correcting or compensating for any disturbance to the system. As this process continues over time, states of limited or partial equilibrium, for instance those of the sensori-motor period, are replaced by 'better' states which are characterized by being able to handle a greater number of contingencies and by being more mobile, more permanent and more stable.

One of the key notions is that improvement in equilibrium is very closely related to the achievement of a greater degree of reversibility. The perfect reversibility of operational thought (section 3.5) is a feature to which Piaget returns again and again. Thus in a length conservation task the child begins by seeing two sticks of equal length exactly aligned. He then sees one of them moved sideways so that the alignment is destroyed. This disturbance is compensated for, however, if the child understands that the movement can be exactly balanced or reversed by a movement in the opposite direction. In this case, the equality is conserved, and equilibrium is maintained.

This kind of stability is held to be developed as a result of processes of equilibration.

4.8 *Equilibration and Learning.* Piaget often discusses the relations between equilibration and learning. For him 'learning' is by no means synonymous with 'development'. Rather, he tends to equate 'learning' with the acquisition of knowledge from some external source – that is, he contrasts it with acquisition as a result of one's own activities. Thus if a child became able to conserve through being told the right answer or through being rewarded when he happened to give the right answer that would certainly be learning. But Piaget believes that no fundamental development takes place in this way. Fundamental developments take place by means of active construction and self-regulation.

Piaget does not rule out the possibility that specific attempts to teach children to conserve and so on may make a difference – particularly if the method is of such a kind as to bring the child up against something which surprises him or causes him to recognize a contradiction. For this experience may call forth new adaptive efforts on the child's part and so set in motion processes of equilibration. However, the possibility that teaching may make a *real* difference will depend on the stage the child has reached: 'Learning is subordinate to the subject's level of development.'

In conclusion, I want to stress again that, in writing this Appendix I have merely tried to give a straightforward account of Piaget's claims, not to evaluate them. The main sources on which the account is based are:

Beth, E. W., & Piaget, J., *Mathematical Epistemology and Psychology*. Dordrecht-Holland: D. Reidel, 1966.

Piaget, J., *The Psychology of Intelligence*. London: Routledge & Kegan Paul, 1950.

Piaget, J., *Logic and Psychology*. Manchester: Manchester University Press, 1953.

Piaget, J., Piaget's Theory. In P. H. Mussen (ed.), *Carmichael's Manual of Child Psychology, Vol. I*. New York: Wiley, 1970.

Piaget, J., *Biology and Knowledge*. Edinburgh: Edinburgh University Press, 1971.

The quotation in section 4.5 is from 'Piaget's Theory', page 710. The quotation in section 4.6 is from *Mathematical Epistemology and Psychology*, page 241. The quotation in section 4.8 is from 'Piaget's Theory', page 716.

References

Anderson, R., Manoogian, S. T., & Reznick, J. S., The undermining and enhancing of intrinsic motivation in preschool children. *Journal of Personality and Social Psychology*, 1976, *34*, 915–22.

Blank, M., *Teaching Learning in the Preschool*. Columbus, Ohio: Merrill, 1973.

Bloom, L., Talking, understanding and thinking. In R. L. Schiefelbusch & L. L. Lloyd (eds.), *Language Perspectives – Acquisition, Retardation and Intervention*. New York: Macmillan, 1974.

Bower, T. G. R., *A Primer of Infant Development*. San Francisco: W. H. Freeman, 1977.

Bower, T. G. R., & Wishart, J. G., The effects of motor skill on object permanence. *Cognition*, 1972, *1*, 165–72.

Bruner, J. S., *Toward a Theory of Instruction*. New York: W. W. Norton, 1966.

Bruner, J. S., The ontogenesis of speech acts. *Journal of Child Language*, 1975, *2*, 1–19.

Bryant, P., & Kopytynska, H., Spontaneous measurement by young children. *Nature*, 1976, *260*, 772.

Campbell, R., & Bowe, T., Functional asymmetry in early language understanding. In G. Drachman (ed.), *Salzburg Papers in Linguistics, Vol. III*. Tübingen: Gunter Narr (in press).

Chomsky, N., *Aspects of the Theory of Syntax*. Cambridge, Mass: M.I.T. Press, 1965.

Clark, E. V., Awareness of language: some evidence from what children say and do. Paper presented at the discussion meeting on 'The Child's Conception of Language', Projektgrüppe für Psycholinguistik, Max-Planck-Gesellschaft, Nijmegen. (To appear in the Proceedings.)

Clark, M. M., *Young Fluent Readers*. London: Heinemann Educational, 1976.

Cole, M., Gay, J., Glick, J. A., & Sharp, D. W., *The Cultural Context of Learning and Thinking*. London: Methuen, 1971.

Deci, E. L., *Intrinsic Motivation*. New York: Plenum Press, 1975.

Donaldson, M., *A Study of Children's Thinking*. London: Tavistock, 1963.

Donaldson, M., & Lloyd, P., Sentences and situations: Children's judgments of match and mismatch. In F. Bresson (ed.), *Problèmes Actuels en Psycholinguistique*. Paris: Centre National de la Recherche Scientifique, 1974.

Donaldson, M., & McGarrigle, J., Some clues to the nature of semantic development. *Journal of Child Language*, 1974, *1*, 185–94.

Douglas, M., *Implicit Meanings*. London & Boston: Routledge & Kegan Paul, 1975.

Downing, J., Children's concepts of language in learning to read. *Educational Research*, 1970, *12*, 106–12.

Fox, B., & Routh, D. K., Analysing spoken language into words, syllables and phonemes: a developmental study. *Journal of Psycholinguistic Research*, 1975, 4, 331–42.

Gelman, R., Conservation acquisition: A problem of learning to attend to relevant attributes. *Journal of Experimental Child Psychology*, 1969, 7, 167–87.

Gibson, E. J., & Levin, H., *The Psychology of Reading*. Cambridge, Mass: M.I.T. Press, 1975.

Grieve, R., Hoogenraad, R., & Murray, D., On the child's use of lexis and syntax in understanding locative instructions. *Cognition*, 1977, 5, 235–50.

Gruber, K. H., Backwards to Europe. *Times Educational Supplement*, 24 June 1977, 18–19.

Hall, L. C., Linguistic and perceptual constraints on scanning strategies: some developmental studies. Edinburgh University: unpublished doctoral dissertation, 1975.

Harris, P. L. (personal communication).

Henle, M., The relationship between logic and thinking. *Psychological Review*, 1962, *69*, 366–78.

Hewson, S. N. P., Inferential problem solving in young children. Oxford University: unpublished doctoral dissertation, 1977.

Hopkins, G. M., letter to Robert Bridges dated 17 May 1885. In Abbott, C. C. (ed.), *The Letters of Gerard Manley Hopkins to Robert Bridges*. London: Oxford University Press, 1935.

Hughes, M., Egocentrism in pre-school children. Edinburgh University: unpublished doctoral dissertation, 1975.

Hughes, M., & Grieve, R., Interpretation of bizarre questions in five and seven-year-old children. (In preparation.)

Inhelder, B., & Piaget, J., *The Early Growth of Logic in the Child: Classification and Seriation.* London: Routledge & Kegan Paul, 1964.

Inhelder, B., Sinclair, H., & Bovet, M., *Apprentissage et Structures de la Connaissance.* Paris: Presses Universitaires de France, 1974.

Johnson-Laird, P. N., Legrenzi, P., & Sonino Legrenzi, M., Reasoning and a sense of reality. *British Journal of Psychology*, 1972, *63*, 395–400.

Jung, C. G., The Development of Personality. *Collected Works*, *Vol. 17*. London: Routledge & Kegan Paul, 1954.

Karmiloff-Smith, A., & Inhelder, B., If you want to get ahead, get a theory. *Cognition*, 1975, *3*, 195–212.

Kendler, T. S., & Kendler, H. H., Experimental analysis of inferential behavior in children. In Lipsitt, L. P., & Spiker, C. C. (eds.), *Advances in Child Development and Behaviour, Vol. 3*, 1967.

Lee, L., *Cider with Rosie.* London: The Hogarth Press, 1965 (p. 50).

Lepper, M. R., Greene, D., & Nisbett, R. E., Undermining children's intrinsic interest with extrinsic rewards: A test of the 'over-justification' hypothesis. *Journal of Personality and Social Psychology*, 1973, *28*, 129–37.

Lewis, C. S., *That Hideous Strength: a Modern Fairy Tale for Grownups.* London: Bodley Head, 1945.

Lloyd, P., Communication in pre-school children. Edinburgh University: unpublished doctoral dissertation, 1975.

Macrae, A. J., Meaning relations in language development: a study of some converse pairs and directional opposites. Edinburgh University: unpublished doctoral dissertation, 1976.

McGarrigle, J., & Donaldson, M., Conservation accidents. *Cognition*, 1974, *3*, 341–50.

McGarrigle, J., Grieve, R., & Hughes, M., Interpreting inclusion: a contribution to the study of the child's cognitive and linguistic development. (In preparation.)

McMichael, P., Self-esteem, behaviour and early reading skills in infant school children. In J. F. Reid & H. Donaldson (eds.), *Reading: Problems and Practices* (2nd edition). London: Ward Lock Educational (1977).

Macnamara, J., Cognitive basis of language learning in infants. *Psychological Review*, 1972, *79*, 1–13.

Maratsos, M. P., Non-egocentric communication abilities in preschool children. *Child Development*, 1973, *44*, 697–700.

Olson, D. R., Culture, Technology and Intellect. In L. B. Resnick (ed.), *The Nature of Intelligence*. Hillsdale, N. J.: Lawrence Erlbaum Associates, 1976.

Papoušek, H., Individual variability in learned responses in human infants. In R. J. Robinson (ed.), *Brain and Early Behaviour*. London: Academic Press, 1969.

Piaget, J., *The Language and Thought of the Child*. London: Routledge & Kegan Paul, 1926.

Piaget, J., *The Child's Conception of Number*. London: Routledge & Kegan Paul, 1952.

Piaget, J., *The Child's Construction of Reality*. London: Routledge & Kegan Paul, 1958.

Piaget, J., *The Grasp of Consciousness*. London: Routledge & Kegan Paul, 1977.

Piaget, J., & Inhelder, B., *The Child's Conception of Space*. London: Routledge & Kegan Paul, 1956.

Piéraut-Le Bonniec, G., *Le Raisonnement Modal*. The Hague: Mouton, 1974.

Plato, *Protagoras and Meno*. Translated by W. K. C. Guthrie. London: The Penguin Classics, 1956.

Reid, J. F., Learning to think about reading. *Educational Research*, 1966, *9*, 56–62.

Reid, J. F., & Low, J., *Link-up*. Edinburgh: Holmes McDougall, 1972.

Resnick, L. B., Task analysis in instructional design: Some cases from mathematics. In D. Klahr (ed.), *Cognition and Instruction*. Hillsdale, N. J.: Lawrence Erlbaum Associates, 1976.

Richards, I. A., *How to Read a Page*. London: Routledge & Kegan Paul, 1943.

Rose, S. A., & Blank, M., The potency of context in children's cognition: An illustration through conservation. *Child Development*, 1974, *45*, 499–502.

Satire on the Trades. Translated by J. W. Wilson; in J. B. Pritchard (ed.), *Ancient Near Eastern Texts*. Princeton, N.J.: Princeton University Press, 1955.

Sayers, Dorothy L., *Have His Carcase*. London: Victor Gollancz, 1971 (p. 112).

Siegler, R. S., Three aspects of cognitive development. *Cognitive Psychology*, 1976, *8*, 481–520.

Slobin, D. I., & Welsh, C. A., Elicited imitation as a research tool in developmental psycholinguistics. In C. A. Ferguson & D. I. Slobin (eds.), *Studies of Child Language Development*. New York: Holt, Rinehart & Winston, 1973.

Szasz,,T. S., *The Second Sin*. London: Routledge & Kegan Paul, 1974.

Trevarthen, C., Communication and cooperation in early infancy: A description of primary intersubjectivity. In M. Bullowa (ed.),

Before Speech: The Beginnings of Human Communication. London: Cambridge University Press (in press).

Vygotsky, L. S., *Thought and Language*. Cambridge, Mass: M.I.T. Press, 1962.

Wallington, B. A., Some aspects of the development of reasoning in preschool children. Edinburgh University: unpublished doctoral dissertation, 1974.

Wason, P. C., & Johnson-Laird, P. N., *Psychology of Reasoning: Structure and Content*. London: Batsford, 1972.

Werner, H., *Comparative Psychology of Mental Development*. New York: International Universities Press, Inc., 1948.

Whitehead, A. N., Technical education and its relation to science and literature. In A. N. Whitehead (ed.), *The Aims of Education*. London: Williams & Norgate, 1932.

Ziff, P., *Understanding Understanding*. Ithaca, N.Y.: Cornell University Press, 1972.

Index